# THE HISTOR

## OF THE

# 6TH (SERVICE) BATTALION
# LINCOLNSHIRE REGIMENT

## 1914 - 1919

Merry Christmas 2012
Matthew.

lots of love

Aunt Wena

## COLONEL F.G. SPRING

*From little towns in a far land we came,*
*To save our honour and a world aflame.*
*By little towns in a far land we sleep;*
*And trust that world we won for you to keep!*

*- Rudyard Kipling*

First published in 2008 by Poacher Books.
Copyright © Jonathan Čapek. All rights reserved.

ISBN 978-0-9559914-1-7

Printed by lulu.com
www.lulu.com/poacher_books

# CONTENTS

# ILLUSTRATIONS

Cover Illustration - Captain Hansen wins the Victoria Cross [Courtesy of the Museum of Lincolnshire Life]

1. Officers of the 6th Lincolns prior to embarkation. [Editor's collection]

2. A group of 6th Lincolns take time out from training. [Courtesy of Mrs. J. Adams]

3. Dinner time for the men. [Courtesy of Mrs. J. Adams]

4. A group photo of Lance Corporals, probably taken at Brocklesby Camp. [Courtesy of Mrs. J. Adams]

5. The landing at Cape Helles. [Simpson, C.R., *The History of the Lincolnshire Regiment 1914-1918,* p. 142]

6. Suvla Bay. [Ibid., p. 144]

7. Captain Percy Howard Hansen V.C., D.S.O., M.C. [Editor's collection]

8. The attack on Ismail Oglu Tepe. [Simpson p. 153]

9. The Battle of Messines. [Ibid., p. 251]

10. Brigadier-General Sir Henry Gater. [Editor's collection]

11. The Second Battle of Arras, 1918. [Simpson p. 355]

12. Sergeant Evans wins the Victoria Cross [Ibid., p. 356]

13. Map of the Marquion area. [Ibid., p. 365]

14. Sketch map from Captain Hansen's notebook [TNA WO 95/4299]

15. Arthur Evans V.C., D.C.M. [Editor's collection]

16. Captain Hansen wins the Military Cross. [Courtesy of the Museum of Lincolnshire Life]

# BATTLE HONOURS
## OF THE
# 6TH (SERVICE) BATTALION
# LINCOLNSHIRE REGIMENT

"SUVLA," "Landing at Suvla," "Scimitar Hill,"
"Gallipoli, 1915," "Egypt, 1916" "SOMME, 1916,"
"Flers-Courcelette," "Thiepval," "MESSINES, 1917"
"YPRES 1917," "Langemarck, 1917," "Poelcapelle" "Arras, 1918,"
"Scarpe, 1918," "Drocourt-Quéant," "HINDENBURG LINE,"
"Canal du Nord" "Cambrai, 1918," "Sambre,"
"France and Flanders, 1916-18"

# PREFACE

At the outbreak of the Great War in August 1914, the Lincolnshire Regiment was composed of five battalions - typical of a rural county regiment:

1st (Regular) Battalion - stationed in barracks at Portsmouth
2nd (Regular) Battalion - on garrison duty in Bermuda
3rd (Special Reserve) Battalion - based in Lincoln
4th (Territorial) Battalion - based throughout South Lincolnshire
5th (Territorial) Battalion - based throughout North Lincolnshire

Within twenty-four hours of the Declaration of War, the Secretary of State for War, Lord Kitchener, called for the army to increase in strength by half a million men - thus doubling the size of the Army at a stroke. Two days later a recruitment campaign began which appealed for the first stage of this increase, famously known as the 'First Hundred Thousand'. Volunteers from all over Lincolnshire flooded into recruitment centres across the county, as a tide of patriotism swept the country. The 6th Battalion was born out of this initial enthusiasm and became the first new 'Service' Battalion of the Lincolnshire Regiment to be raised. The 'Lincolns' eventually grew from five battalions to a total of nineteen battalions, eleven of which saw active service in the front-line. Each of these eleven battalions served exclusively on the Western Front except for the 6th, which holds the distinction of having also served five months in the Dardanelles.

The story of the 6th Battalion is perhaps no more remarkable than any other battalion of the British Army during the First Word War but nevertheless, its story remains an important part of the social history of the county from which it was raised. This account of the Battalion represents the most comprehensive narrative of its service during the War, especially given that the Battalion War Diary for Gallipoli Campaign was lost. The original manuscript was written by Colonel F.G. Spring, probably during the mid 1920's, and is thought to have been based on the diary kept by Captain R.H. Clay M.C. For whatever reason, the manuscript was never published at the time, and has only recently been rediscovered. Now, 90 years on from the Armistice, as the war fades from living memory, this history is published here for the first time.

November 2008

# HOME SERVICE

*8 August 1914 – 30 June 1915*

The 6th Service Battalion, Lincolnshire Regiment was one of the first battalions of Kitchener's Army to be raised, and also the first Service Battalion of the Lincolnshire Regiment. It was formed during the first week of the War when, on August 8th 1914, Captain and Lieutenant Jones, two regular officers of the Lincolnshire Regiment, arrived at Belton Park near Grantham, to make preparations for receiving recruits from the Depot at Lincoln, where they were already enlisting in large numbers.

Two Companies, 'A' and 'B', were formed at first and by the end of the month numbers had increased to such an extent that two additional companies, 'C' and 'D', were added, and the original nucleus of a few regular soldiers had grown into a battalion. Lieut.-Colonel Phelps was in Command, Major Wilkinson Second in Command, Lieutenant Hansen Adjutant and Lieutenant Jones Quartermaster. The Company Commanders were: 'A' Company Captain Elkington; 'B' Company Captain Browne; 'C' Company Major Fraser; 'D' Company, Captain Norton. Major Wilkinson stayed with the Battalion only a very short time, and when he left, Captain Elkington assumed the appointment of Second in-Command, whilst Lieutenant Croydon D.C.M., formerly R.S.M. to the Battalion, took over Command of 'A' Company.

The Battalion was raised in the 33rd Infantry Brigade, of the 11th Division, composed chiefly of troops recruited in the Midlands. Other battalions in the 33rd Infantry Brigade were the 6th Border Regiment, 7th South Staffordshire Regiment and 9th Notts & Derby Regiment (Sherwood Foresters).

Our own battalion contained a fair sprinkling of regular officers, whilst the men were of the best natured in the country. Recruited chiefly from Lincolnshire, a large proportion were agricultural workers, already accustomed to an outdoor life and very fit. The physical standard for troops in these days was high and the physique of our men was wonderfully fine.

The Battalion was quartered in tents in Belton Park, just outside Grantham, and for the first few months the men wore ordinary civilian clothes, or the temporary uniform which was issued pending a supply of the regulation khaki being available. Training started with very elementary drill and musketry, varied by many route marches and much physical training. No rifles were available for Musketry, and target practice was carried out with air guns on a miniature range.

The autumn of 1914, one long unbroken spell of sunshine, was ideal for training and the men soon learnt the rudiments of soldiering. In November, a large camp of huts, which had been in the course of preparation, was completed, and the Battalion moved from the tents to the new quarters. All training had hitherto been in Companies but it was now succeeded by Battalion and later by Brigade training and field days. A Rifle Range was completed and firing took place very frequently with the available rifles.

*Fig. 1: Officers of the 6th Lincolns prior to embarkation. Starting at the back and working left to right, the officers are as follows: 2/Lt. R.L. Hornsby, Lt. F.S. Cannell, Lt. A.P. Snell, Lt. H. Sargent, Lt. K.J.W. Peake, Lt. G.C. Downes, 2/Lt. R.G. Ingle, 2/Lt. D. Akenhead, Lt. L. Webber, 2/Lt. T.D. Overton, 2/Lt. A.S. Hemsley, 2/Lt. J.C. Foster, 2/Lt. A.H. Bird, 2/Lt. L.J. Lill, 2/Lt. G.M. Hewart, Capt. A. Hoade (Staff Capt., 33rd Infantry Brigade), Major W.E.W. Elkington (Sec.-in- Command), Brig.-Gen. R.P. Maxwell (G.O.C., 33rd Infantry Brigade, Lt.-Col. Phelps (Commanding), Capt. F.G. Spring (Brigade Major, 33rd Infantry Brigade), Major A.E. Norton, Lt. H. Winslow-Woollett.*

Concerts were organised, mainly by the Adjutant, to entertain the men during the winter evenings.

In March 1915 the Division was moved to Salisbury Plain. The Battalion marched from Grantham, via Melton Mowbray and Thurmaston to Lutterworth, where it entrained for Farnham. On arrival, the Battalion, with other units of the 33rd Infantry Brigade, was stationed in a camp at Frensham, the other Brigades in the Division being at Whitley.

More advanced training was carried out, and consisted chiefly of Battalion, Brigade and Divisional field days. The Battalion reached a high state of

*Fig 2: A group of 6th Lincolns take time out from training to pose for a photograph. Three of the men can be seen wearing the topee helmets of the Mediterranean Expeditionary Force. L/Cpl. Harry Brewer is stood far right.*

efficiency and officers and men grew very impatient at being kept in England.

In June the Battalion was reviewed by The King, and soon afterwards orders to prepare for active service were received. On June 30th 1915, the Battalion entrained at Frensham and proceeded to Liverpool to embark for service with the Mediterranean Expeditionary Force.

*Fig. 3: Dinnertime for the men.*

*Fig. 4: A group of Lance Corporals, probably taken at Brocklesby Camp.*

# GALLIPOLI

## *1 July 1915 – 1 February 1916*

On July 1st 1915 the Battalion embarked at Liverpool on the *Empress of Britain* and sailed the same day. The other three Battalions of the Brigade and Brigade H.Q. were also on board. The Battalion embarked at full strength, except for the Transport Section, which was left behind in England. The following officers proceeded with the Battalion:

Battalion Headquarters
O.C.                             Lieut.-Colonel P. Phelps
2nd in Command         Major W.E.W. Elkington
Adjutant                   Captain P.H. Hansen
Quartermaster           Lt. P.H. Jones
Medical Officer         Lt. Clark, R.A.M.C.

'A' Company
O.C.                             Captain A.C. Croydon D.C.M.
2nd in Command         Lt. F.S. Cannell
No.1 Platoon            Lt. G.C. Downes
No.2 Platoon            Lt. D. Akenhead
No.3 Platoon            2/Lt. R.L. Hornsby
No.4 Platoon            2/Lt. G.M. Hewart

'B' Company
O.C.                             Captain P.L. Browne
2nd in Command         Lt. L.O. Wickham
No.5 Platoon
No.6 Platoon            2/Lt. T.O. Overton
No.7 Platoon            2/Lt. A.S. Hemsley
No.8 Platoon            2/Lt. T.G. Parkin

'C' Company
O.C.                             Major D'A. M. Fraser
2nd in Command         Captain J.T. Lewis

| | |
|---|---|
| No. 9 Platoon | 2/Lt. J.K. Murphy |
| No.10 Platoon | Lt. H. Winslow-Woollett |
| No.11 Platoon | 2/Lt. R.L. Cook |
| No.12 Platoon | Lt. C.H.A. French |

'D' Company

| | |
|---|---|
| O.C. | Major A.E. Norton |
| 2nd in Command | Captain F.P. Duck |
| No.13 Platoon | Lt. K.J.W. Peake |
| No.14 Platoon | 2/Lt. A.H. Bird |
| No.15 Platoon | 2/Lt. R.D. Foster |
| No.16 Platoon | Lt. L. Webber |

| | |
|---|---|
| Machine Gun Officer | Lt. A.P. Snell |
| Transport Officer | Lt. H. Sargent |

When required:

| | |
|---|---|
| Signalling Officer | Lt. C.H.A. French |
| Scout Officer | 2/Lt. R.L. Hornsby |

Fine weather was enjoyed during the whole of the voyage, which despite the ever-present danger from enemy submarines, was a most enjoyable one. After passing through the Straits of Gibraltar, khaki drill was issued. The *Empress of Britain*, escorted the whole way by three destroyers, and after stopping at Malta for coal, arrived in Alexandria Harbour on July 12th. At Alexandria a stay of four days was made for surplus stores to be unloaded. The Record Office personnel were left at Alexandria. Officers and senior N.C.O.s were granted leave to visit the town, and each day the Battalion carried out a short march to exercise the men.

Leaving Alexandria on July 16th the *Empress of Britain* sailed northwards, through the Aegean Sea, dotted with countless rock islands, and dropped anchor in Mudros Harbour on July 18th.

Two days later the Brigade transhipped into small river steamers, and on arriving near Helles, the southern point of the Gallipoli Peninsula, was transferred to trawlers, which discharged their human freight on the *River Clyde*, the historic ship which had been such an historic part in the original landing at Cape Helles, and was now stranded on the beach near Sedd el Bahr. The

Brigade came under the orders of G.O.C. Naval Division, and two days later the Battalion moved into the front line before Achi Bara, relieving a battalion of the Naval Division. The French were on our immediate left.

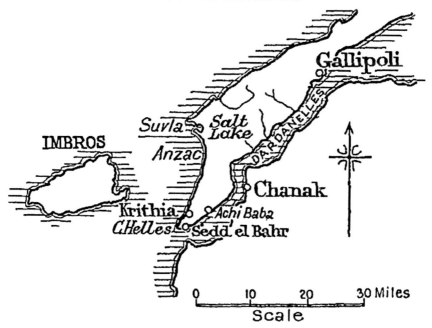

*Fig. 5: The landing at Cape Helles.*

Officers and men were all very keen and anxious for an opportunity of getting to grips with the enemy. Trenches were in a very bad state, exposed in many places to the fire of enemy snipers, and only half completed. The men at once set to work deepening and improving them. The Turks kept up a continual rifle fire, very accurate and deadly, but our own snipers soon set to work to alter matters. In those days a man took great interest and pride in his rifle, and took every opportunity for a shot at the enemy. The chief feature of the Gallipoli campaign, all through, was the rifle fire. Not only was one subject to it in the firing line, but back on the beach in Reserve, which was never out of range from rifle fire. Many casualties were caused by the dropping bullets, which the Turks systematically fired in the air over our lines. The first casualty in the Battalion was caused by long range rifle fire, Company-Quartermaster-Sergeant Wrightson being hit on July 22nd whilst coming up the line from the beach. Second Lieutenant Overton, the first officer casualty, was killed a day or two

13

later by a bullet through the head.[1]

After a week in the line, the Battalion went back into Reserve on the beach, still under heavy shell fire. Two days later we returned to the line, and on the night of August 1st/2nd were relieved by French Senegalese troops, and re-embarking, were taken to Imbros, where were waiting the other two Brigades, who had come directly from England.

This fortnight in the line was a great asset to the Battalion in the heavy fighting which was to follow. The men had got over the first nervousness of being under fire, the sensation of seeing a comrade killed, and had become inured to the hardships of fighting conditions. In fact, they had acquired self-confidence, and were ready to go anywhere and to do anything. Casualties had been light but dysentery already had started to claim its victims.

It was then announced that the whole Division would very shortly take part in the landing at Suvla Bay, just North of where the Australian and New Zealand troops had already established themselves at Anzac Cove, the object being to advance, and joining up with the Australian forces, rush into the eastern coast of the Gallipoli Peninsula, thus cutting off the Turkish troops opposing our troops to the South. Embarking and disembarking from lighters was practised in the harbour at Imbros.

On the afternoon of August 6th the Battalion embarked on a destroyer, the other Battalions of the Brigade embarking on destroyers and lighters, and as it grew dark we set forth to take part in the heaviest fighting the Battalion has ever experienced.

The 33rd Infantry Brigade landed on 'B' beach, a mile and a half South East of Nibrunesi Point at 11.30 p.m. Beyond a few shots from Turkish snipers, who quickly withdrew, no opposition was encountered. The 7th South Staffords, the 9th Sherwood Foresters landed first, followed by Brigade Headquarters, and then our own Battalion and the 6th Border Regiment. The 7th South Staffords, the 9th Sherwood Foresters took up a line from the South East corner of the Salt Lake, and came under the orders of Divisional Headquarters, whilst the remainder of the Brigade, with the 6th East Yorkshire Regiment (Pioneers) were in Divisional Reserve. Our orders were to be at the junction of

---

[1] T/Lt. Thomas Darwin Overton was killed in action on 30th July 1915, aged 21. He was the second son of the Reverend Canon Frederick Arthur Overton and Ella Overton of The Rectory, East Barnet, Hertfordshire. Educated at Winchester College (1908-13) and New College, Oxford (entered 1913). When war was declared in August 1914 he was mountaineering in Switzerland but immediately returned home to receive a commission. He is buried in Redoubt Cemetery, Helles (Sp. Mem. B. 121).

the Azmak Ravine with the Anafarta Sagir - Suvla Point road at dawn. The 34th Infantry Brigade was to land on the Northern shores of Suvla Bay, obtain possession of the high ridge of Karakul Dagh, and established themselves on Chocolate Hill by dawn. The 32nd Infantry Brigade had been ordered to land on

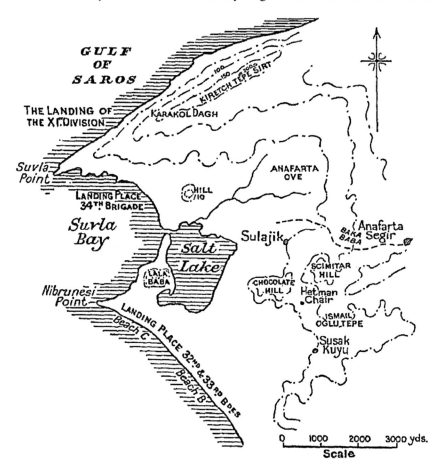

*Fig 6: Suvla Bay.*

the beach South of Suvla Bay, opposite the Salt Lake, secure Lala Baba, a hill between the Salt Lake and the sea shore, and then follow the 34th Infantry Brigade.

We followed the 32nd Infantry Brigade, skirting the eastern slopes, which had been taken by the 6th Yorkshire Regiment. The Salt Lake on our right at the time was dry, was about two square miles in extent, and was separated from the sea by a narrow strip of land along which we were now proceeding in a Northerly direction. Above this strip of land a small inlet, also dry, connected the Salt Lake with the sea. When halfway along the strip of land towards the inlet, fighting could be seen taking place on the far side of the latter. The day was breaking, and the Battalion, which, with Brigade H.Q., was leading, began to come under rifle fire from Turks on the Northern shores of the Salt Lake.

The men, who, owing to the bad-going over the rocky ground, were extended a long way back, were ordered to dig in. Then the Turks began shelling fairly heavily with guns on the ridge north of Suvla Bay. Casualties would have been heavy but for the soft bed of the Salt Lake partially smothering the burst of the shells.

During the morning the 10th Division was seen landing West of Lala Baba, and passing over the inlet north of the Salt Lake.

At 2 a.m. the following afternoon - August 7th - orders were received that we were to advance in support of the 31st Infantry Brigade (10th Division) who were attacking Chocolate Hill. We were to be supported by the 6th Border Regiment.

'C' and 'D' Companies started off immediately in artillery formation, supported by 'A' and 'B' Companies, and passed along the northern shore of the Salt Lake. Shortly afterwards, orders were received that the 10th Infantry Brigade having failed, the Battalion, supported by the 6th Border Regiment, was to take Chocolate Hill.

The advance continued in extended order, under heavy shrapnel fire but the men went on without flinching, as steadily and as regularly as if they were carrying out a field day. Two hundred yards from the foot of the hill, and seven hundred yards from the summit, the Battalion came across the Royal Dublin Fusiliers, 10th Division, and halted under cover. 'D' and 'B' Companies advanced through the Dublin Fusiliers by short rushes. Major Norton was hit at this time, and Captain Duck took over command of 'D' Company. Companies became more or less split up owing to casualties, the heavy fire which was being directed on them, and the small parties of Dublin Fusiliers scattered about under cover.

Companies were quickly re-organised and reformed, whilst 'B' and 'D' Companies prepared for the assault. Leaving the Dublin Fusiliers behind, the Battalion advanced in short rushes under heavy fire. One hundred yards from the crest, 'B' and 'D' Companies made a last halt of half an hour, whilst our

16

artillery and machine guns played on the Turkish positions above.

Then the charge was ordered, and with a rush, our men carried the Turkish trenches on the top of the hill. Many Turks were bayoneted or shot whilst they were running away. A communication trench running down the reverse slope of the hill enabled a few Turks to get away but most of them were killed.

Captain Duck and Lieutenant Webber of 'D' Company were the first to cross the enemy trenches. Lieutenant Webber unfortunately was shot dead whilst crossing the trench, into which he fell. The positions were consolidated and prepared against enemy counter-attacks and whilst this work was proceeding, the Royal Dublin Fusiliers came up.

The losses in the fight were five Officers and 164 Other Ranks. Major Fraser and Lieutenant Webber were dead, Major Norton, Second Lieutenants Bird and Hemsley were wounded. So ended the first, and perhaps the finest attack ever carried out by the Battalion. After a whole brigade had attacked Chocolate Hill, and had failed, the Battalion, unaided, went straight at it and took the hill.[2]

The 6th Border Regiment had co-operated on our left, and afterwards pushed out to the eastern slopes of the hill. During the night Chocolate Hill was taken over by the 31st Infantry Brigade and we went back in the early morning of August 7th to Divisional Reserve at Lala Baba.

On the afternoon of August 8th, instructions were received that the Brigade, less the 9th Sherwood Foresters, and with the assistance of two battalions of the 31st Infantry Brigade, which would be attached to our own Brigade, would attack the Anafarta Ridge between and exclusive of Anafarta Sagir and Ismail Oglu Tepe, a hill 300 feet high, 14,500 yards South West of Anafarta Sagir. Brigadier-General Maxwell took the Commanding Officers on to Chocolate Hill and pointed out the objective, and orders for the attack were then issued. The attack was to be carried out with the 6th Border Regiment on the right and 7th South Staffordshire Regiment in the centre and our own battalion on the left. One of the two attached battalions, the 6th Dublin Fusiliers, was ordered to move up behind the 7th South Staffords and support them, or the flank battalions as required. The machine guns of the two attached battalions were brigaded under our Brigade Machine Gun Officer to form a right flank guard for the Brigade and advance on Ismail Oglu Tepe. One of our own

---

[2] More information on the landing at Suvla Bay and the attack on Chocolate Hill is provided in Postscripts I - IV.

two machine guns had been damaged at Cape Helles and could be neither replaced or repaired. The Battalion, therefore, went into action with one machine gun only.

The Battalion was to deploy behind Hill 70, called Scimitar Hill, situated north-east of Chocolate Hill, and 2,200 yards from the objective. This hill was supposed to be held by British troops.

At 2 a.m. on August 9th the battalion left the bivouacs near Lala Baba, and proceeded along the north side of the Salt Lake, to Chocolate Hill, where a halt was made for the 7th South Staffordshire Regiment to come up. Hardly had the troops begun to move forward from Chocolate Hill when heavy rifle fire was opened up from the northeast and at the same the enemy time began to shell Chocolate Hill. It afterwards transpired that the troops holding Hill 70, behind which the Battalion was to deploy, had been withdrawn during the night, and the Turks advancing had occupied Hill 70.

The Battalion therefore immediately deployed at 4.10 a.m. into two lines of half battalions, on a front of 500 yards. 'A' Company on the right was supported by 'D' Company, and 'B' Company on the left was supported by 'C' Company and the advance commenced against Hill 70. Already it was very doubtful whether the battalion could reach the final objective - Anafarta Ridge. With Hill 70 held by the enemy, there was a very stiff task ahead, before the original programme could be started.

Officers and men, realising the situation, went forward undaunted. Troops of the 32nd Infantry Brigade were coming back across our front but the Battalion pushed on steadily and after severe fighting drove the Turks off Hill 70. Whilst the position was being consolidated a strong counter-attack began to develop. 'D' Company was forced to turn half left to meet this attack and further advance became impossible. The enemy were in large numbers, and our casualties became very heavy but the men put up a stubborn fight and held on steadily. The 7th South Staffordshire Regiment on our right was hard pressed and, through heavy casualties, a gap opened up on our right between ourselves and the Staffords.

The two battalions of the 31st Infantry Brigade were sent up to help us but did not make any headway. The Territorial Battalions, which had landed that morning began to arrive, a Company at a time, but did far more harm than good. On reaching our line, and coming under heavy fire, they rushed back. Several times the C.O., Adjutant and Captain Duck managed to stop these parties and send them back to the firing line.

During the whole of the morning our men held on to the hill, fighting stubbornly. But for their gallantry, the Turks would have broken through and have swept through to the beach. The ground in front of our line was strewn with Turkish dead but our own casualties had been very heavy.

The hill top was covered with dry gorse and bushes which several times during the morning had been set on fire by the shelling. Just before mid-day a large fire started just in front of our line. It quickly spread and drove our men back. The air was black with smoke, blinding the men, and all the time the Turks poured on a heavy fire. With no alternative, the Colonel, at 12.15 p.m., gave the order to withdraw and the Battalion fell back on a trench 300 yards in rear, bringing back as many wounded as possible. The new position was consolidated but the crest of the hill was never regained.

It was then that Captain Hansen, calling for volunteers, went out with four men, 400 yards in front of our line into the burning scrub and under heavy rifle fire, rescued six wounded from the terrible death of being burnt. For this action Captain Hansen was awarded the Victoria Cross.[3]

---

[3] The award of the Victoria Cross to Captain Hansen was officially announced in the London Gazette on 1st October 1915 and presented to him by the King on December 4th. L/Cpl. A.H. Breeze who went out with Captain Hansen was awarded the Distinguished Conduct Medal. See Appendix II for their official citations.

*Fig.7: Captain Percy Howard Hansen V.C., D.S.O., M.C.*

Captain Duck and Captain Croydon had also done very fine work[4]. Casualties that day were terrible, the worst the Battalion had ever suffered in a single attack. Of the officers who went into action that day, only five, the C.O., Adjutant, Captain Duck, Lieutenant Jones (Quartermaster) and Lieutenant Clark (Medical Officer), were unscathed. Of the men, only 120 to 130 came out of action.[5] Other battalions in the Brigade lost nearly as heavily. On Brigade H.Q., the Brigade Major, Captain (afterwards Brigadier-General) F.G. Spring and the Brigade Signalling Officer, had been wounded.

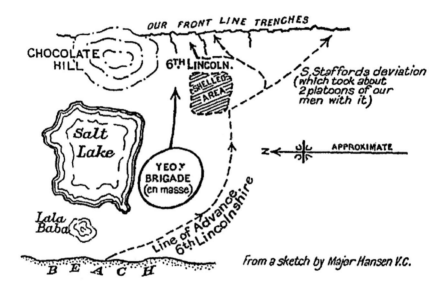

*Fig. 8: The attack on Ismail Oglu Tepe.*

The following day the 53rd Division renewed the attack on Anafarta Ridge.

---

[4] For their part in this action, Captain Duck was awarded the Distinguished Service Order and Captain Croydon received the Military Cross. Their official citations are provided in Appendix II.

[5] The Battalion suffered 12 officers killed, wounded and missing and 391 rank and file, out of a possible 17 officers and 561 other ranks. According to the Regimental History the officers killed were Captains P.L. Browne and J.T. Lewis, Lieutenants T.G. Parkin, G.M. Hewart, K.J.W. Peake, R.L. Cook. Missing, presumed killed were Lieutenants R.D. Foster and R.L. Hornsby. Wounded: Major W.E.W. Elkington, Captain A.C. Croydon and Lieutenant C.H.A. French. Lieutenant G.C. Downes was wounded on the 7th in the attack on Chocolate Hill and died of his wounds on the 11th. None of the men recorded as missing were ever seen again.

We were to co-operate in the attack and move on to Ismail Oglu Tepe. But Hill 70 was never retaken, though two attacks were delivered by the 53rd Division in the morning and again in the afternoon, so we were ordered to hold on to the trenches we had consolidated the previous night.

On August 12th we were relieved by the 34th Infantry Brigade and went down to the beach for a rest. The Battalion was so weak that it was reorganised into two companies. Shortly afterwards we again went into the line and remained there until the night of August 20/21st, when we were relieved by the 29th Division and again went down to the beach.

A general advance all along the line from Anzac to Suvla was ordered for August 21st. The 33rd Infantry Brigade in Divisional Reserve at Lala Baba was ordered to advance round the South side of Chocolate Hill and seize Ismail Oglu Tepe. The formation adopted was each battalion in artillery formation in the order, 9th Sherwood Foresters, 6th Border Regiment, 7th South Staffordshire Regiment, 6th Lincolnshire Regiment. The advance started from Lala Baba soon after 3.00 p.m. and shortly afterwards a whole division of dismounted Yeomanry suddenly appeared from the South East corner of Lala Baba, in mass or close column, broke through the 7th Staffords and eventually turned at right angles and made for the western slopes of Chocolate Hill. The appearance of this thick body of troops brought down heavy artillery fire, which started a fire in the bush.

The result of the Yeomanry breaking through the Brigade, and of the fire, which the troops had to go out of their course to avoid, was that part of our battalion and the 7th South Staffords lost direction and moved too much to the right. The loss of direction was never checked, and these troops eventually finished up with the 34th Infantry Brigade, well to our right. The Turks were holding a strong redoubt on the plain of Hetman Chair, five to six hundred yards South East of Chocolate Hill. The Sherwood Foresters attacked this position, getting within a few yards, but lost very heavily in doing so, their Commanding Officer and Second in Command being hit.

The Borders then came into the attack but could make no headway, their Commanding Officer being killed. Had it not been for the unfortunate loss of direction mentioned above, the redoubt would have been taken. The remaining Company of our Battalion was kept in Brigade Reserve. Meanwhile things were not going well elsewhere. The 29th Division and Yeomanry on our left suffered heavy casualties and were brought to a standstill before Hill 70. Units were by this time badly mixed up and no further advance was made. The following morning, the Turks, after a violent bombardment, counter-attacked but were driven back. On the night of the 22nd/23rd August we were relieved by a Brigade of the 10th Division. Casualties had again been very heavy. With the exception of our own C.O., all the senior officers in the Brigade had become casualties.

After a short period in the trenches round Chocolate Hill, we went over to the extreme left of the line on to the high ridge of Karakul Dagh, North of Suvla Bay. The strength of the Brigade at this time, including reinforcements, was only nineteen officers and 1,546 Other Ranks, and the four battalions were amalgamated into two battalions. We, with the 6th Border Regiment formed a composite battalion under our own Commanding Officer, Lieut.-Colonel Phelps, with Captain Hansen as Adjutant.

Our own battalion took over-the line at Kiretch Tepe Sirt, astride the high ridge, of which the culminating point was Jeffson's Post. The ground was very hard and rocky, and the trenches very bad. Under two foot of soil was the solid rock, impossible to penetrate, so the trenches were in many cases breastworks, insecure against the Turkish rifle fire. Of dig-outs there were none. Rough bivouacs were constructed by digging out a square hole and covering it with a waterproof sheet. Much hard work was necessary before the trenches were at all secure.

Dysentery quickly became very prevalent and was continually reducing the numbers. Everyone suffered from it. All stores had to be carried by hand from the beach up to our positions, and this made a very heavy demand on the strength of the men, already weakened by dysentery. The arrival of an Indian Mule corps somewhat relieved the situation but great hardship was suffered by the scarcity of water. Trench warfare began, and continued without break until the evacuation. On September 10th Lieut.-Colonel Phelps went off with dysentery. Captain Hansen became Commanding Officer, combining his new duties with those of Adjutant. A fortnight later he too succumbed to dysentery, and Captain Cannell, who had commanded the remnants of the 7th South Staffordshire Regiment, was recalled to command our own battalion.

The Battalion had little rest. Coming back to the beach for a periodic rest, every available man would be employed trench digging, road making, digging winter shelters in the mountainside, carrying parties and innumerable other working parties.

On October 17th Major G.H. St. Hill of the North Devon Hussars arrived and assumed command of the Battalion, Captain Cannell becoming Adjutant.

Large reinforcements were frequently received but neither officers nor men withstood for long the hardships of life in Gallipoli, and most of them succumbed sooner or later to dysentery.

On October 20th the Brigade went back to the beach for a rest, which however was no rest, as the men were called upon to do twelve hours hard work a day.

In the middle of November the Battalion took over a section of the line on the extreme right of the Divisional Front, and this section was held by the Brigade until the evacuation.

Up till this time the weather had been very hot and settled but on November 20th a terrible blizzard was experienced. Torrents of rain fell and completely flooded the trenches. Several men were drowned. A large number of men sheltered in small excavations in the cliff side over the beach and were swept away down to the sea and drowned. The Turks suffered just as badly, and enmity was forgotten in fighting the elements. The torrential rain turned to snow, and was followed by nine degrees of frost. Officers and men with no adequate shelter suffered terribly. After getting wet to the bones and then having to endure severe frost, over a hundred men went down with frostbite.

At the beginning of December, rumours of an impending evacuation to the Peninsula by our troops began to circulate but work in our trenches was continued on our defences as hard as ever. Much wiring was done, and a line of posts called the 'Grouse butts', in front of our line, was under construction. Many casualties from rifle fire occurred in carrying out this work, which in the bright moonlight exposed our men to accurate fire from the Turkish posts.

The evacuation of Suvla Bay was carried out on the night of December 20th/21st. For some time previously, stores had been quietly removed and embarked, and as many men as possible were sent off on the night of December 19th/20th. Our Battalion was holding the front line on the last night. A party consisting of Captain Burrows, Second Lieutenants Sutherland Foster, Donald and Jones with twenty-seven picked N.C.O.s and men, was detailed as rearguard for the Battalion. Fixed Battalion collecting points were established, and the Battalion marched down to the embarkation centre on the beach, leaving behind the rearguard, known as the "last ditchers". At the embarkation centre numbers were checked, and the Battalion embarked on lighters as accommodation became available.

All our artillery, with the exception of a few worn out 18-pdrs., had been withdrawn, and all stores which could not be got away were collected into large dumps on the beach and soaked in petrol ready for lighting when the time came.

The rearguard moved from the front line at a fixed time, leaving behind a few lights, fires and contrivances for firing rifles at intervals. The party withdrew to the second line, closing gaps in our wire entanglements as they left. Similar procedure was adopted on passing through the third line of defences, and the rearguard finally arrived on the beach and embarked. The Turks had no idea of what was happening. The whole Battalion embarked without a casualty. Major-General Fanshawe, commanding the 11th Division was the last to leave Suvla Bay.

Before the last lighters left, all the dumps were lighted, and the Turks at once began to shell them heavily. The huge fires, throwing up dense volumes of smoke, and lighting up the sky for miles around, formed a most impressive spectacle for the thousands of troops as they slowly moved across to Imbros. It was with intense thankfulness that everyone left Gallipoli, the scene of heavy but fruitless fighting, where many brave men had lain down their lives to no avail.

On arrival at Imbros at 9 a.m. on December 21st we found a camp prepared for us by our advance party and quickly settled into it. Major St. Hill returned to his own regiment, and Major Elkington came from Egypt and took over command of the Battalion. The next five weeks were spent in training. Bombing and signalling classes were held, and musketry was carried out on an improvised range.

On January 28th the Battalion embarked on the *Princess Alberta* and left Kelphales Bay, arriving in Mudros Harbour the same day. There the Battalion re-embarked on the *Tunisian*, which on January 30th sailed for Egypt.

# EGYPT

*2 February 1916 – 7 July 1916*

The Battalion disembarked at Alexandria from the *Tunisian* on February 2nd, 1916, and marched to Ramleh Station and thence proceeded by train to Sidi Bishr Camp. Sidi Bishr Camp for many months had been the station of the 'details'. Picturesquely situated on the sandy expanse of gentle undulations, it seemed a veritable fairyland after many months on the barren rocks of the Aegean. The camp was a scene of continual activity. Nearly every Division in the Mediterranean Forces was represented in the vast area of tents, which covered many miles extending to the sea shore. The long, white, dusty roads, which seemed to reflect the scorching rays of the sun, were lined on either side as far as the eye could see, with the booths of the native vendors, who filled the air with their invitations to buy. Gaily caprisoned donkeys, pursued by shrieking Arabs, bore the soldiers to and fro between the camps and the tram terminus. In the very centre of the plain rose a sun-bleached mosque.

Amidst these surroundings the Battalion quickly settled down, tents being pitched on the Western side of the Alexandria - Aboukir Railway. A few days were spent getting the camp ship-shape, and then training was commenced in earnest. After the comparatively cool weather in Imbros, the heat seemed rather considerable but not oppressive, and it was occasionally varied by rain which, once it started, came in earnest. Training was rather intensive. There was physical drill for half an hour before breakfast, followed by three hours training in ordinary drill and attack practices during the morning, finishing up with Musketry and lectures for two hours in the afternoon. Added to this, night operations were carried out once or twice a week. The open sandy plains, dotted with occasional palm groves, provided an ideal training ground but the heat and the heavy going made it thirsty work, and by evening everyone was very tired, but not too tired however, to enjoy the numerous and varied attractions of Alexandria.

In a very short time, the afternoon parade developed into a bathing parade, to everyone's relief. The coast at Sidi Bishr is generally rocky but there can be found many sandy bays sheltered from the waves, delightful for bathing. Altogether the stay at Alexandria has always been considered the pleasantest period in the history of the Battalion. Doubtless the sudden change from isolation and hardship to civilization and comparative comfort intensified life's pleasure, and invested it with a particular glamour which still remains in recalling these days.

On February 6th Lieut.-Colonel M.P. Phelps rejoined from sick leave and assumed command of the Battalion from Lieut.-Col. Elkington, who took over the duties of Second in Command. Early in March, orders were received that the Division would shortly relieve another Division then holding the outpost line east of the Suez Canal, between Port Said and Ismailia. Preparations for the move were regretfully made, and on March 9th 'A' and 'B' Companies entrained at Sidi Gaber, under Major Elkington, together with the Battalion Transport Section, which had been reformed a week or two previously under Major (then Second Lieutenant) Sutherland D.S.O., M.C. This party detrained at Ballah the following day and there awaited the remainder of the Battalion, which arrived early on the morning of March 11th. The Canal was crossed by a swinging pontoon bridge operated by personnel of the Egyptian Labour Corps, whose weird chants aroused much wonder.

The policy at this time was a passive one in the Sinai Peninsula. During the previous year the Suez Canal itself had been the line of defence, but in view of the policy of the Turks repeating their attempt to cross the Canal, a system of fortified works, covered by outposts, had been thrown out in the desert about six or eight miles east of the Canal. These systems of fortified works were under construction to cover the whole length of the coast, with a lateral interval of six to ten miles between each system. It was to one of these systems, which was being taken over by the 33rd Infantry Brigade, that the Battalion was proceeding. Ballybunion, the name bestowed on this system by the Australian troops who started it, was not at this time in a very advanced state of construction. The road, which was intended to connect it with Ballah, only existed for two miles from Ballah, after which there was merely a track over the sand. To escape the heat of the day, the Battalion left Ballah about 6.00 a.m. and arrived at Ballybunion about three hours later. The men were not yet accustomed to carrying full marching order over the loose sand, and found the march very tiring. To make matters worse, when two miles from Ballah a sandstorm suddenly arose. Ballybunion was found to be a small camp in one of the countless mullahs, surrounded by half-dug trenches. It did not show to advantage that day.

The Brigade was disposed with two battalions, the 6th Lincolns and 7th South Staffords holding Ballybunion and its outposts; the 6th Borders and 9th

Sherwood Foresters in reserve on the eastern bank of the Canal at Ballah, where Brigade H.Q., the various Q.M's Stores and Transport Sections were also situated.

On arrival at Ballybunion, 'B' Company was pushed out to Post 64, a small defensive work on a low sandhill, three miles north out of Ballybunion. The following day, an additional outpost position was taken up by 'A' Company at the Punch Bowl, a sandhill three miles due east of Ballybunion. Outposts of the 7th South Staffords covered Ballybunion on the South East. Two Companies 'C' and 'D', therefore remained at Ballybunion, and at once commenced work on the trench system in course of construction. The loose sand made this work very difficult, and it was found necessary to revet the trenches with hurdles covered with rushes and anchored to sandbags. The 68th Field Company, Royal Engineers organised and supervised the work. Often, after a trench was completed, one of the anchor wires would snap and the whole thing would collapse, rendering futile the work of many days. At other times, sandstorms would fill the trenches so that they were barely discernable, and the sand would have to be patiently dug out again. The trenches were generally sited just behind the crest of a sandhill, with a comparatively small field of fire of one or two hundred yards. They were mutually supporting and altogether protected the camp on all sides. In front were several thick belts of wire, gapped in various places for communication, completely surrounding the camp.

As the month proceeded, the heat in the day gradually grew more intense and work on the trenches was restricted to early morning and late afternoon and evening. The two Companies on outpost duties were employed in much the same manner as the two Companies at Ballybunion. During the day they continued the construction of defensive works, at night time holding an outpost line in the usual manner with sentry groups and picquets. They were connected by telephone to Battalion H.Q.

Life under these conditions was not unpleasant but tended to become very monotonous. The water supply was a great problem. Water could only be obtained from a pumping station at Ballah on the west bank of the Canal, being pumped from the fresh water canal at Ismailia, fifteen miles further south. From Ballah it was carried in the tanks used by the natives, called fantasies, by camel convoys. Camels were the only means of transport between Ballybunion and Ballah, and all stores, including rations, had to be brought up by this means. The amount of water that could be carried was necessarily very limited.

A man very rarely received more than two quarts a day for washing and drinking, a great hardship under the conditions. Happily this state did not last for very long. The road from Ballah was quickly pushed on till it reached Ballybunion, and passing through it turned off to the South towards El Ferdan. With the completion of the road, motor lorries replaced the camels; a short time after a light railway also connected Ballybunion with Ballah. Water pipes were laid next, ensuring a plentiful supply of water, and Ballybunion began to lose its forlorn aspect. Rush huts were built as Mess rooms for the men, canteens were started, other improvements were made until finally Ballybunion took on an appearance of the usual Army camp.

The monotony of working continually on the trenches was occasionally broken by field days, Battalion or Brigade, in which the two companies at Ballybunion would deliver attacks on the outpost companies, or defend their own positions against attacks from the battalions at Ballah. Leave for the officers to visit Cairo or Alexandria was given, though very sparingly, yet the change it provided was very welcome.

A battery of 18-pdrs. of the 59th Brigade Royal Field Artillery was stationed at Ballybunion, and at times the infantry had to take cover whilst the guns ranged on various objects beyond the outposts. The precautions ordered for this artillery practice have since seemed ridiculously absurd. Not a soul was allowed to approach within a mile and a half of the objects at which the guns were firing, very different from keeping within thirty yards of a barrage. But guns in those days were not the familiar objects they are now. They were indeed looked on with awe, unknown and dreaded.

Life on the outposts was rather enjoyed. The junior officer would be in charge of his own platoon post, rarely visited by a senior or staff officer. It was a care-free life, provided with plenty of amusement by the mule supplied to each outpost company as officer's charger, pack animal, in fact for transport purposes generally. Major-General Fanshawe, dressed very unobtrusively, quite unattended, would occasionally visit the outposts and hold animated discussions regarding the sitting of trenches with subalterns, who were under the impression that they were conversing with the Quartermaster of a neighbouring unit.

Occasionally, after sunset in the gathering dusk, a dainty little gazelle would be seen on the skyline, head uplifted, sniffing for a possible enemy, or peacefully nibbling the tufts of thick coarse grass scattered over the desert. Many were the attempts made to approach within rifle shot of these wary creatures but never with any success.

Of Turks, no sign was ever seen. The Yeomanry patrols, which were sent

28

out daily through the outpost line, would frequently chase small bands of Arabs but the horses, unused to the soft, yielding sand, were no match for the swift camels. The only prisoner ever brought in was a little Arab girl, wandered from a passing caravan. The strong Turkish attacks delivered in the Katia district in April did not extend so far south as Ballybunion, though Turkish patrols must have passed very close to our outposts under cover of the heavy mist which prevailed all that day.

Early in April, Captain C. Hutchinson, afterwards familiarly known as "Pukka Hutch", joined the Battalion from the 7th South Staffordshire Regiment and took over the duties of Adjutant from Captain F.S. Cannell, who assumed command of 'A' Company.

On April 27th Lieut.-Colonel Phelps left the Battalion sick; Major Elkington taking over command and re-assuming the rank of Lieut.-Colonel. Captain Cannell became Second in Command.

On May 13th there was an inter-battalion relief. The Battalion, after relief by the 6th Border Regt. marched to Ballah to a camp on the east of the Canal. This change was very welcome to everyone. With the Canal so near at hand, bathing was at once very popular. The midday heat was getting rather intense and, for the fear of sunstroke, bathing was forbidden between the hours of 10 a.m. and 4 p.m. Except during these hours, the whole Battalion always seemed to be in the water, and many impromptu water carnivals were held. Work on the defence at Ballah was continued. Owing to the heat it was not possible to work during the daytime. From 10 a.m. to 4 p.m. each day not a soul could be seen in the camp, save a solitary sentry sheltering from the sun in the shade of an awning. As the work on the defences at Ballah was by this time almost completed, more and more attention began to be given to training. Several Brigade field days and night marches with attacks at dawn were practiced, sometimes with the co-operation of the 34th Infantry Brigade at El Ferdan.

Towards the end of May leave to Port Said was opened for the men, providing them with some welcome diversion. By the beginning of June the heat in the daytime was often getting almost unbearable. Sometimes the hot winds bearing sand from the Sahara would sweep across the Canal. Men would lie naked in their tents, almost stifled. But these did not last for long. Usually, about midday when the heat was worst, a cool refreshing wind from the Mediterranean would blow gently down the Canal.

At this time the Battalion was up to full strength in men, and well over strength with regards officers. A big draft had joined the Battalion on its arrival in Egypt, and officers were continually joining from the Base Depot at Alexandria. The Regimental Transport had been brought to a high state of efficiency, which it has for ever afterwards maintained. Officers and men were all very fit and full of high spirits but there came into being a longing for change. Other Divisions had been sent to France, and rumours were continually arising that the 11th Division was going to France also. Everyone gradually became obsessed with the idea of going to France, except a few men who had been there.

On June 12th Captain A.C. Croydon M.C., D.C.M. rejoined the Battalion from England, and took over Second in Command from Captain F.S. Cannell, who re-assumed command of 'A' Company. Rumours still persisted that the Division would leave Egypt at an early date, and finally orders were received to this effect. On July 1st 1916, the Battalion entrained at Ballah, after being relieved by the 8th Royal North Lancashire Regiment (42nd Division) and arrived at Alexandria Docks early the following morning. Embarkation took place at once on H.M. Transport *Huntspill*, which sailed the same afternoon.

The Battalion embarked with a strength of thirty officers and 952 Other Ranks. At that time battalions proceeding to France were not allowed to take more than thirty officers. In consequence, ten officers who had been serving with the Battalion in Egypt were left at the Base Depot at Alexandria to their great disappointment.

Whilst in Egypt, Vickers Guns had been withdrawn from Battalions and Brigaded as Machine Gun Companies, being replaced in Battalions by Lewis Guns.

Keen as all ranks were to get to France, it was with many regrets that they saw the sunlit shores of Egypt fade in the distance. Egypt with its pleasant care-free life, where war at that time was only a make believe sort of game, was the scene of what is generally considered the pleasantest period in the Battalion's history. And it was with mixed feelings that men turned their faces to France, where, after a respite of six months, they would renew their acquaintance with the grim realities of war.

The *Huntspill* was not a comfortable boat. She was too narrow in the beam to remain steady in any kind of a sea, and chancing to run into a choppy sea immediately on leaving Alexandria Harbour, nearly everyone on board was violently seasick for the first twenty-four hours, after which they grew more or less accustomed to the whimsical rollings of the ship. A French corvette asked as escort, and the voyage to Marseilles was accomplished without incident, except for a fright one night off Malta, when an enemy submarine, which had sinister designs on the *Huntspill*, mistook the escort for the troopship to everyone's relief.

# FRANCE

## *8 July 1916 – 5 September 1916*

On July 8th the *Huntspill* steamed slowly up the wide bay of Marseilles, past the historic Château d'If, coming to rest at a quay in the harbour. The softly shaded green of the steep hills, which rise to the North of Marseilles, gave a wonderful restful feeling after the glaring sands of Egypt. The six days which the men had spent cooped up on board left them very soft. It was curious to see the dragging, shuffling step acquired by marching over the loose sand. The Battalion disembarked the following day, stayed two nights at a rest camp in Marseilles, and on 11th July entrained for the British Army Zones.

After a pleasant journey lasting three days up the Rhone valley, through Lyon, thence through Macon, Chalon-sur-Saone, Versailles, Amiens and Abbeville, the Battalion arrived at Saint Pol, where it detrained and marched late into the night to billets at Ternas. Leaving Ternas the following day, the march was continued to Hauteville, some 18 km west of Arras. It was then heard that the Battalion was to go into the line almost immediately, South East of Arras. Company Commanders and N.C.O.s from each Company went to reconnoitre the section of the line to be taken over, and a platoon from each company was sent up in advance.

On July 20th the Battalion marched to Berneville, three miles South West of Arras, and two days later relieved a battalion of the Ox & Bucks Light Infantry. The section of the line taken over was astride the Arras-Beaurain-Bapaume Road, opposite the strongly fortified village of Beaurain. A wide front of 2000 yards was held by three companies, 'C' under Captain Burrows on the right, 'A' under Captain Cannell in the centre and 'B' under Captain Akenhead on the left, with 'D' Company under Captain Thompson in Reserve at Ronville. This part of the line had been taken over from the French only a short time before, and the trenches were in a very unsatisfactory condition. Deep dugouts were unknown. Except for occasional bombardments by heavy trench mortars, particularly on the right company's front which sometimes caused a fair number of casualties, everything was very quiet.

The first casualty in France was No. 12862 Pte. Sambrooks of 'D' Company, slightly wounded by shrapnel on July 21st. The first man to be killed was No. 9293 L/Cpl. Rose of 'C' Company shot through the head whilst looking over the top opposite the quarries near Beaurain Road. The first officer casualty was Second Lieutenant Wilkinson, shot through the calf in a patrol skirmish. Inter-company reliefs took place every ten days.

Looking back on this period one chiefly remembers the poppies. The ground was scarlet with them, and they were found everywhere, even in the trenches. The line ran through many gardens and often did men crawl out regardless of risk to search for strawberries and raspberries. A Light Trench Mortar Battery was formed in the Brigade and the subalterns of 'A' Company particularly delighted in strafing the enemy's posts and watching the stakes and barbed wire fly heavenwards. Second Lieutenant Blagden of the Battalion, second in command of the Trench Mortar Battery, was a born Stokes gunner. His intense interest and enthusiasm in this often despised weapon was astonishing. Every night as it was growing dusk, Major Croydon, escorted by a diminutive runner, could be seen carefully threading his way along the tortuous trenches, calling at Company H.Q. for the latest news, and occasionally for a drink.

Leave at this time was closed but Captain Cannell, with his usual resource, discovered urgent private affairs, which called for his immediate presence in England, and he applied for Special Leave. Soon afterwards an orderly called at 'A' Company's H.Q. in the line and Captain Cannell, clad in pyjamas, received the glad tidings that his leave was granted. It is stated by those who should know, that he dressed and was at Battalion H.Q. before the orderly, who went straight back to Battalion H.Q.

At this time identification of the enemy holding the line opposite the Battalion Sector was urgently required by the Higher Command in connection with the Somme battle, which was raging 20 km further south, and into which the Battalion was destined to be thrown. On the night of August 9th/10th, Captain (then Second Lieutenant) R.H. Clay with his platoon, and Sergeants North and Sleight of 'C' Company, carried out a raid on an enemy sap, known as 'Y' Sap. The original intention was to cut through the wire at the base of the sap, enter and capture a post at the forward end of the sap. This was in progress, and the party was nearly through the wire when Second Lieutenant Clay discovered, by the light of the flares, an enemy wiring party forty yards to the right of the sap. He withdrew his party, and reforming it in a line with the flanks pushed well forward, advanced on the enemy working party from a flank. Before getting near enough to rush the working party, the raiders were discovered and fired on by an enemy covering party, whose presence was suspected. The raiders replied with rifle fire and bombs, then rushed the covering party and inflicted casualties on the working party. No prisoner was taken unhurt but two wounded ones were taken back, both dying on reaching our lines. One slightly wounded Boche could not be extricated from the wire into which he had rushed, and was left there with three dead. Thus, six casualties were inflicted on the enemy without loss to the raiding party. Badly needed identifications were obtained, and congratulatory messages were received from Army, Corps, Division and Brigade.

On August 13th Lieut.-Colonel Elkington left to rejoin his old Battalion, the 1st Lincolnshire Regiment, and Major G.H. Gater D.S.O. of the 9th Sherwood Foresters assumed command in his place.

After a month in the line, on August 21st the Battalion was relieved by the 5th Royal Berkshire Regiment and proceeded to Berneville, staying there the night, and marching to Hauteville the following day. It was then announced that after a short period of intensive training, the Battalion would be put into the Somme fighting. Training commenced immediately, and for a week was probably the stiffest the Battalion had ever done. Starting at 6 a.m. with short intervals for meals, it lasted till 5 p.m. and was carried out, except for lectures, in full marching order. The Battalion was then suddenly moved to Houvin-Houvigneul, a small village south of Saint Pol, where training was continued another two days.

On September 2nd the Battalion entrained at Brevent, detraining at Acheux, directly behind the Somme fighting, and marched to Lealvillers, a small village nearby. A big Casualty Clearing Station was situated in this village, where came the wounded from a big attack on September 3rd. Their stories of the fighting were eagerly listened to, for it was realized that in a few days the Battalion would, after many months, again be involved in desperate fighting. The suspense of waiting at Lealvillers was not long protracted.

On September 5th the Battalion marched to Bouzincourt, four miles from Thiepval, the enemy's great stronghold.

# THE SOMME BATTLE

*6 September 1916 – 3 October 1916*

The Somme battle had been raging for over two months. Considerable success had attended the continual attacks south of Albert, and the enemy's positions had been penetrated to a depth of five or six miles. But at the Northern end, the seemingly impregnable stronghold of Thiepval, crowning the summit of a steep hill which rises from the valley of the Ancre, had successfully resisted all attacks. So long as Thiepval was in enemy hands the whole advance was held up. Little imagination was required to realise what the Battalion would shortly be "up against".

The whole of the Brigade was in Bouzincourt, with the exception of the South Staffords, who went straight into the line. Civilians were still living in Bouzincourt, which was shelled very frequently. A little training was attempted but could not be carried out regularly owing to the demands for working parties near the line, and the shelling, which caused five casualties. Second Lieutenant Smith and Sergeant Tighe were wounded whilst on a working party[6]. Early on the morning of September 12th, the Battalion relieved the 9th Sherwood Foresters in the line near Ovillers, a mile and a half south of Thiepval. 'B' Company took over the right of the line, with 'D' Company on the left. 'C' Company were in Support with 'A' Company in Reserve in Ovillers. It was whilst this relief was in progress that the Battalion had its first experience of gas shells, which the enemy was using freely. Being lachrymatory gas, although causing some discomfort, no one was seriously injured. On the right of the Battalion was a Canadian battalion and on the left the 6th Border Regiment, which had relieved the 7th South Staffordshire Regiment.

A week or so previously the enemy had been driven from Ovillers and Pozieres, and was at this time holding a line roughly east and west through Mouquet Farm. Our own front line ran more or less parallel with the enemy's, at a distance varying from 70 yards to 300 yards. Both ourselves and the enemy were holding, as far as possible, what remained of the old enemy trenches. The

---

[6] 6137 Sergeant John Tighe died of haemorrhage following his wounds on 24th September 1916. He is buried in Grimsby (Scartho Road) Cemetery, Lincolnshire (grave ref. 68. A. 23).

policy in those days, on either side, was to hold a fixed line continuously, in strength, and neither attacks nor defences were organised in depth as they came to be later. The consequence was that both our own and the enemy's front lines were literally packed with men, having posts every fifteen yards or so. The trenches were almost obliterated, and the bombardment was continuous. Casualties were inevitably heavy.

The following day the Battalion H.Q. moved up from Ovillers to a Battle H.Q., and in the evening the 32nd Infantry Brigade, on the left of the 33rd Infantry Brigade, delivered a surprise attack on the "Wunderwerk", the southern bastion of the Thiepval defences. The attackers started before their own barrage and fairly caught the enemy unprepared. After a short fight, the "Wunderwerk" was taken and, unprotected on the south; it was evident that Thiepval would not much longer hold out. Retaliation during this attack was somewhat heavy on the Battalion front, and among other casualties, Second Lieutenant Marsh was wounded. Sergeant Handsley did very fine work at this time holding for forty-eight hours an isolated post, for the purposes of retaining touch with the Canadians on the right. For this he was awarded the Military Medal.

Fortunately, there were a fair number of deep dugouts in which to take shelter from the shelling. The scene was one of utter devastation. At Ovillers, not a wall was standing, hardly a brick was visible, so thoroughly had our big guns done their work. Pozieres was much the same but Mouquet Farm, held by the enemy, contained several large undamaged cellars.

The whole countryside had been so incessantly ploughed up by shells that not a blade of grass was visible. Yet the methods of the enemy's artillery in those days was rather crude. A valley in front of Ovillers was full of our guns in action. There were literally thousands, but never a shell was fired at them by the enemy's artillery. This may be partially accounted for by the complete mastery of the air, which we had at this time, but the general tendency was for artillery to concentrate almost entirely on the forward area, making it very unpleasant for the troops in the line.

The Canadians on our right attacked and took Courcelette just before dusk on the 16th, meeting with complete success. Second Lieutenant Clay was wounded whilst pushing out to a sap to keep in touch with their left flank in front of Mouquet Farm. Later in the evening the Battalion was ordered to clear Constance Trench, which ran obliquely from our line to the enemy's, and the greater portion of which was held by the latter. Second Lieutenant Donald successfully cleared this trench with a bombing party, and it was occupied by

'C' Company. During the night the enemy made a counter-attack with bombs on Constance Trench but was driven off. Second Lieutenant Stockdale was killed during this attack, and Second Lieutenant Malkinson was wounded. Altogether the Battalion suffered fifty casualties that night, and the previous day twenty-three men, working under Lieutenant Playle, had been hit by one shell. Captain Akenhead was severely wounded by a shell.

A patrol sent out by the left Company – 'D' Company failed to return, and Captain Thompson went in search for it after daybreak. Several hours went by and the patrol came in, having had to take cover in shell holes from an enemy machine gun for three hours, but Captain Thompson did not return. Second Lieutenant Sutherland very gallantly went in search of Captain Thompson, and found his body, where he had been killed by an enemy sniper from a post only fifty yards away. With considerable difficulty, Second Lieutenant Sutherland got back, and that night he brought Captain Thompson's body into our own lines. For this he was later awarded the Military Cross. Captain Foster then assumed command of 'D' Company.

On September 19th the Battalion was relieved and moved back into Support at Donnets Post near Aveluy. It had been a trying week, during the whole of which the Battalion had been subjected to intense shell fire, many casualties had occurred and everyone was thoroughly exhausted. Lt-Colonel Gater D.S.O. had done very fine work, going constantly round the line and encouraging the men, regardless of danger. The Battalion remained in dugouts at Donnets Post for a week, resting and supplying working parties.

On September 26th, the 6th Borders and 9th Sherwood Foresters, taking part in an attack on a wide front, attacked and captured Joseph's Trench. Thiepval and Mouquet Farm were taken on this day. The Battalion was in support for this attack, for which carrying parties were supplied. Second Lieutenant Ingersoll was killed. The next day the Battalion moved up into the line, taking over Stuff Redoubt, a maze of trenches, the northern portion of which was held by the enemy. The weather, which up to this time had been fine, suddenly broke, and rain came down continuously, adding to the discomfort of the men.

'C' Company under the leadership of Captain Burrows, gallantly held Stuff redoubt against several counter-attacks, during which Captain White of the Yorkshires won his Victoria Cross and Captain Burrows gained the Military Cross. The enemy was fighting very stubbornly and was making desperate efforts to regain Stuff Redoubt which, however, remained in our hands. On

September 30th, the Battalion was relieved by the 8th Loyal North Lancashire Regiment, having suffered over seventy casualties during its last tour in the line, and marched back through Bouzincourt to Hédauville, where it stayed the night, continuing the march to Lealvillers the following day.

From Lealvillers to Heuzecourt the men were taken in lorries and, on October 3rd they marched into Gramont, the final destination of the Rest Area. Although the Battalion had not taken part in any big attack during this fighting, several minor operations had been carried out, and all ranks had behaved splendidly during a prolonged period of strenuous effort, hardship and exposure to heavy shell fire.

# BEAUCOURT AND GRANDCOURT

*4 October 1916 – 24 March 1917*

G ramont, where the Battalion was resting, was a small village, eighteen miles east of Abbeville, situated in well wooded, undulating country, very suitable for training. Six weeks were spent there in re-organizing and training. Major S.J. Burnett joined the Battalion and assumed the appointment of Second in Command in the place of Major Croydon, M.C. D.C.M., who had proceeded to the Senior Officer's School, Aldershot. Captain Hutchinson left the Battalion to take up an appointment as Instructor at the 5th Army School. Second Lieutenant Pattinson became Acting Adjutant.

Time passed very rapidly at Gramont. The Battalion left on November 14th, and marched to Hédauville, breaking the journey at Fieffes and Vadencourt.

The attack by the Naval Division on the Ancre had taken place three days previously, and it was naturally supposed that the 11th Division was being brought up to take part in these operations. In one day, Saint Pierre Diyion, Beaumont Hamel and Beaucourt had fallen and the opportunity seemed a great one for exploiting this success. But conditions had changed entirely since the Battalion had last been in the line. The weather had quite broken up, rain had been falling almost daily during the past month and the valley of the Ancre was a sea of liquid mud. After several false alarms, the Battalion, on the 21st November, marched up to a ravine between Beaumont Hamel and Beaucourt, where it was in support to the 7th South Staffordshire Regiment and 6th Border Regiment, holding Beaucourt. Bivouacs were quickly constructed, and the Battalion remained there four days, supplying working parties for the front line battalions. The road from Hamel to Beaucourt was a nightmare one can never forget. A high bank on one side, and the River Ancre on the other, preventing anyone from leaving it, however hard it might be shelled. And well the Boche knew it. All his guns seemed to be concentrated on this one road, which they got in direct enfilade. The spot where the road from Beaumont Hamel joined this road, near Hamel Station, received most attention.

All day long, and all night long, 5.8's with a long drawn shriek would come down with a crump right in the road, or in the marshes just beyond. And by some evil chance this spot was just at the end of the ravine where the

Battalion was living. But by lying very low, casualties were only light. The road itself hardly deserved to be dignified by being called a road. It might have been at one time but then it was simply a morass, often knee-deep in mud and full of shell holes hidden by the mud, and containing many gruesome objects. Boche limbers, dead mules, dead Boche and a few of our dead.

On November 24th the Battalion relieved the 7th South Staffords in the line and the following day received a draft of 103 Other Ranks, many of whom saw their first and last of the war at Beaucourt. At that time we were holding the Northern Bank of the Ancre, a mile East of Beaucourt, and just opposite Grandcourt, which the enemy was holding. Thence our line swung back westwards, a square copse called Bois d'Hollande being inclusive to us, to within 600 yards of the northern outskirts of Beaucourt, where the line again turned North. The Battalion was holding the Eastern portion of the line, with the 6th Borders on the left, Battalion H.Q. was in an old Boche trench dugout in Beaucourt, right on the main road. The weather was bad, and the shelling was unprecedented (for us) in its intensity. We had eighty casualties whilst holding this line for four days. Second Lieutenant Sutherland again greatly distinguished himself.

The line was advanced northwards about 300 yards, the Colonel himself pushing out the posts. Never were officers or men more ready for relief than they were November 28th when the 8th Duke of Wellington Regiment (32nd Brigade) relieved us and we went back to Forceville near Acheux.

The Battalion remained at Forceville resting until December 9th when it moved up to Englebelmer to Brigade Reserve. The Brigade had taken over from the 34th Infantry Brigade a front immediately south of Ancre River and in front of Grandcourt. The 6th Border Regiment took over the right front, the 9th Sherwood Foresters were on the left, and the Lincolns and South Staffords were in Reserve in Englebelmer. Brigade HQ were situated under a steep bank near the river on the edge of Thiepval Wood.

Then began a period of holding the line, which lasted until the middle of January 1917. The Battalion worked with the 6th Borders doing eight days in the line and eight out at Englebelmer. The part of the line the Battalion used to hold was very uninteresting, consisting chiefly of mud and shell holes. The ground was too badly cut up and water logged, for trenches at be dug, though several ineffectual attempts were made. Thiepval, which lay in the Battalion's area, was in the usual state of desolation, though it contained many deep dug-outs, which were much appreciated.

40

At first, when the enemy were expecting a renewal of our attack, things were fairly lively but gradually they quietened down and life became very monotonous. Work there was in abundance, such as draining dug-outs, constructing duckboard tracks. A very creditable piece of work by Sergeants Harrison and Burton, for which they were each awarded the Distinguished Conduct Medal, is the only incident worth relating. On the night of January 3rd/4th an enemy patrol captured two prisoners of the Gloucesters on our right, and was returning when a burst of artillery fire caused the patrol to venture too near one of our advanced posts under Sergeants Harrison and Burton, who rushed out alone, attacked the patrol, of which they captured four, and released the two Gloucesters.[7]

Englebelmer, where the periods of rest were spent, was hardly prepossessing in appearance. The civilian inhabitants had long ago been evacuated, the village was very frequently shelled, and many of the buildings had been destroyed. Those which remained were in a very dilapidated and tumbledown state. The men slept in any old buildings with a roof, and the officers were little better off. Rats were there in swarms. Every building was full of them, and rat catching was the chief amusement of the officers and men.

It might be worth adding that the first concert party to be seen by the Battalion was at Englebelmer, and the first Battalion concerts in France were held there. Empty beer barrels formed the stage, and the performance always consisted of the pathetic songs the British Tommy knows so well.

The time at Englebelmer could hardly be called a rest. We were living in discomfort, and the days were spent in working on the roads, yet everyone kept surprisingly cheerful. We were in the line on Christmas Day but were relieved in the evening, and managed to spend a jolly Christmas.

About this time Major Croydon M.C. returned from England but did not remain long with the Battalion, being appointed to command a Battalion of the West Yorkshire Regiment. Lieutenant Clay was appointed Adjutant on January 1st 1917; Lieutenant Pattinson having proceeded on a staff course.

Casualties during this period were light: Second Lieutenant Wincott, who had done very valuable work with the Battalion, was wounded in the face and arm by a shell splinter, and eventually lost one eye.

On January 19th the Battalion was relieved by a battalion of the Naval Division. Up to a few days previous to this, the weather had been extremely

---

[7] See Appendix II for the Distinguished Conduct Medal citations of Sergeants Burton and Harrison.

wet.  After a heavy fall of snow, a very severe frost which lasted many weeks, set in.

The Battalion returned to Englebelmer for the night, going by buses the following day to Puchevillers and thence by route march on succeeding days through Gézaincourt, back to the Gramont area, this time being billeted in two small adjacent villages - Hanchy and Le Festel.  The period that followed was one of intense cold, and many times we thanked our lucky stars that we were out of the line.

Training was carried out very methodically, special attention being paid to range firing and musketry, which up to this time had been somewhat neglected in favour of bombing.

In the middle of February the Battalion was ordered to move to the Authie Valley, east of Doullers, there to carry out railway work under a Canadian Railway Construction Company.  The Battalion marched there, staying one night at Fienvillers, and arriving in the Authie Valley on February 16th Battalion H.Q., 'B', 'C', and 'D' Companies being billeted in Saint Leger, and 'A' Company under Captain J.C.P. Howis in Authie.

Work on the railway which was under construction, was commenced at once, and the men quickly won the approval of the Canadian Engineers by their steady work.  Very little leisure was allowed, work being carried on from 8 a.m. till 4 p.m. daily, including Sundays.  Bathing even was not allowed to interfere with this work.  The frost, which had lasted five weeks, broke suddenly, and the main roads, always bad, became in an indescribable state.  With mud everywhere, the Battalion was ordered to move into tents at Couin, the next village to Saint Leger.  'A' Company moved to Thièvres, where they were fortunate enough to get good billets.  The Battalion with the exception of 'A' Company, returned to Saint Leger on March 8th and the railway was continued.  This was rather dull and monotonous and came to an end on March 24th, when the Battalion moved to Orville, where training was recommenced in earnest.

# THE HINDENBURG LINE

*25 March 1917 – 17 May 1917*

Preparations were then being made for the attack at Arras, which took place at the end of the month. The XVIII Corps, to which the 11th Division was attached, was being held in readiness to push right through Owie, up the enemy flanks, in the event of the attack being a considerable success.

Open warfare was accordingly practised instead of the old trench to trench attacks, which hitherto in France, had formed the whole of the training. Training was intense but enjoyable. Company, Battalion and Brigade schemes were practised, night operations and outposts and various tactical schemes.

The Arras attack took place but was so impeded by the weather, that rather to our relief we were not called upon to carry out the role which had been allotted to us. Just previous to this the enemy had carried out his famous Somme withdrawal.

Battalion sports were held for the first time in France one Sunday afternoon early in April. On April 12th the Battalion commenced moving back to the line. Thiepval, Beaucourt and the valley of the Ancre, the scene of our last fighting, were now twenty miles behind the line, which was now almost in the Hindenburg Line.

The first march was in a heavy snowstorm to Louvencourt, where the Battalion remained a week and continued training. The march was then continued to Bouzincourt, and thence through Albert along the Bapaume Road to Courcelette, where the night was spent in bivouacs. The next day passing through Bapaume, the object of some Somme fighting of the previous year, now only a heap of smoking ruins, the Battalion reached its destination - Haplincourt - a village destroyed by the enemy in his withdrawal, and situated seven or eight miles east of Bapaume. There the Battalion held the old enemy lines of defence, to guard against any attempt by the enemy at a breakthrough, such as had nearly occurred at Lagnicourt a few miles to the North only a week or two previously. The Division was attached to the 1st ANZAC Corps which was then holding this part of the line, and on April 23rd the Battalion relieved the 6th Australian Battalion in the line at Louverval.

Louverval was a small village directly opposite Moeuvres, which has since been the scene of heavy fighting. The attack at Lagnicourt referred to above had extended as far south as Louverval, where it had been successfully held by the 6th Australian Battalion. The enemy were here holding an outpost line, a mile in front of the Hindenburg Line, which ran just west of Moeuvres. Our own positions also consisted of outposts covering a line of resistance just in front of Louverval. Trenches were non-existent. The countryside consisted of big rolling plains, grown over with grass during the enemy occupation, and almost treeless. Except for frequent shelling of Louverval (where Battalion H.Q. was situated in a cellar) with 5.9's, the line was very quiet. The enemy had begun to use his artillery in back areas and in counter battery work, rather than in our own front lines, and our own artillery, which found concealment very difficult, had a rather thin time. Enemy aircraft, with the addition of the Fokker plane, had grown considerably bolder.

Few casualties occurred, and at the end of April the Battalion was relieved by the 9th Lancashire Fusiliers (34th Brigade) and went back to Velu Wood, where a pleasant time was spent under canvas for a week. Velu Wood was a charming spot. It is true there were several 12" howitzers in action there but the chief danger was from the Australian troops who, from morning till night, were shooting with rifles at wood pigeons and rabbits.

On May 6th the Battalion moved up into Reserve behind Hermies, relieving the 8th Duke of Wellington's Regiment. The 9th Sherwood Foresters were in the line on the right, with the 7th South Staffordshire Regiment on the left. The Battalion supplied numerous working parties, and was due to go into the line on May 14th, when the Division was relieved. The Battalion was relieved by the 4th Ox & Bucks Light Infantry, and after marching through Velu, spent the night in huts at Beaulencourt, on the edge of the old Somme battlefield. Thence the Battalion marched on the following days through the Somme battlefield, staying at Montauban and Fricourt, and entrained at Albert on May 17th for Belgium.

# MESSINES

## *18 May 1917 – 18 June 1917*

Editor's Note: a description covering the part played by the 6th Lincolns at the Battle of Messines is missing from the draft of Spring's account of the Battalion. The official report of the action, as documented in Battalion War Diary, is also missing. As a consequence, this chapter has been largely borrowed from *The History the Lincolnshire Regiment, 1914-1918*, by C.R. Simpson, which was itself, primarily based on the diary of Captain R.H. Clay M.C.

The maintenance of pressure on the Arras front, which kept the enemy constantly on the alert, enabled final preparations to be made for the opening of the Flanders offensive, which was to begin with the Battle of Messines.

The actual front selected for this operation extended between nine and ten miles from a point opposite St. Yves to Mount Sorrel. The objective of the attack was a group of hills known as the Messines-Wytschaete Ridge, which lies about midway between Armentières and Ypres. Messines itself is situated on the southern spur of the ridge which commands a wide view of the valley of the Lys and enfiladed the British lines to the south. North-west of Messines, Wytschaete, situated at the point of the salient and on the highest part of the ridge, commanded a view of almost the entire town of Ypres and all the old British positions in the Ypres Salient.

A special feature in the operations due to take place on the 7th of June was one original in warfare - the explosion of nineteen deep mines at the moment of assault. No such mining feat had ever before been attempted. In the construction of these mines, eight thousand yards of gallery had been driven and over one million pounds of explosives used.

Nine divisions were to take part in the actual assault, and three were in support, among which was the 11th Division who latter lay opposite Wytschaete, and in rear of the 16th Division at the centre of the attack.

Having left at Albert on the night of 17th/18th of May, the 6th Lincolns detrained at Caëstre and marched to Le Thieushouck where they were billeted. The first three days at Le Thieushouck were spent in interior economy and company training, although the training was greatly restricted by the highly cultivated state of the surrounding ground. On May 22nd the Division was informed that it was to take part in the coming operations, and two days later the

Battalion marched to a training area situated on the frontier between France and Belgium, about six miles in rear of the Wytschaete sector. The following two weeks where were spent in training for the attack.

The 11th Division received orders to pass through the 16th Division when the latter had captured its objective. The role of the 33rd Brigade was to pass through and capture a trench system three miles east of Wytschaete.

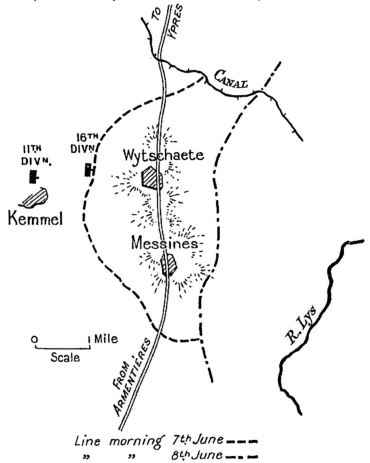

Line morning 7th June ━ ━ ━
    „        „      8th June ━ ▪ ━

*Fig. 9: The Battle of Messines.*

At midday on the 6th of June orders were received to attack the following morning. Preparations were quickly made and at 11.30 p.m. the Lincolnshire marched to Butterfly Farm, two miles from the front line, to await final orders.

As dawn was breaking on the 7th, there was a sudden rumbling of the earth, huge flames shot up, clouds of smoke, dust and debris, a rocking of the ground - as the nineteen mines "went up." Before one was able to regain one's normal faculties, there was another deafening crash as the barrage roared out from a thousand guns. The 6th Lincolns had taken up a position among the "Heavies" and were almost stunned by the ear-splitting din of the monsters as they roared and poured a hail of big shells upon the wretched Germans.

The 6th Lincolns waited in suspense for the first results of the attack. The barrage still continued but at about 9 a.m., word was received that the 16th Division had taken their first two objectives and were pushing on to the third. At about 11 a.m., orders were received to advance to the Vierstraat Switch, a trench running parallel to, and about a thousand yards behind, the British line. At about midday the battalion reached its destination and the men had dinner, while Lieut.-Colonel Gater went to Brigade Headquarters for further orders. Just after 2 p.m., he returned with the information that at 3 p.m., another barrage would fall under cover of which the battalion was to attack the third objective. The forming-up place was to be two miles away on the further slope of the Wytschaete Ridge but the intervening ground was badly cut up by shell-holes, broken trenches and communication trenches full of troops and wounded men. The battalion, being scattered over a thousand yards of trench, had to be got together, and so as not to be late, Battalion Headquarters and 'D' Company started off and arrived at the forming-up line just as the barrage opened. The other companies had not yet come up, so Lieut.-Colonel Gater decided to push on with 'D' Company for fear of losing the barrage. 'D' Company shook out into artillery formation and advanced. Australian troops were on the right and portions of the 6th Border Regiment on the left, with the 7th South Staffords and 9th Sherwood Foresters in support and reserve respectively.

The enemy's artillery opened fire as soon as our barrage fell but his barrage was weak and ill-directed, and many of his guns were effectively smothered by our fire.

'D' Company extended into line in two waves after passing through the first line of posts held by the 16th Division. Very little opposition was encountered: the enemy either ran or surrendered until the objective was nearly reached. Here the Germans attempted a counter-attack but with the assistance of tanks it was broken up, and by 5 p.m. the objective had been gained. Casualties during the attack had been extraordinarily light, 'D' Company losing only two or three men. The heaviest losses were in Battalion Headquarters: Lieutenant F.C.

47

Thorn and Regimental-Sergeant-Major Smith and twenty Other Ranks being wounded.

The senior Company Commander, Captain Howis, brought up the remaining three companies with very few casualties. The appearance of these companies, comparatively fresh and intact, was of enormous value in consolidating the position. As dusk was falling the German guns began to shell the position heavily. Captain Sutherland was wounded in the face, and a platoon of 'C' Company, holding a strong point, was entirely wiped out (with the exception of and Lieutenant Read, who was badly wounded).

Early next morning on the 8th, another counter-attack developed which at one time looked serious until A Company, with Lewis gun and rifle-fire, succeeded in breaking it up. Second Lieutenant Rowlands was wounded and 'A' Company had altogether about a dozen casualties. One N.C.O. - Sergeant Biggadike - was conspicuous for his bravery; he died very gallantly, successfully maintaining his post which the enemy attempted to rush.[8]

Lieut.-Colonel G.H. Gater was wounded in the face when leading 'D' Company to the attack but with great self-sacrifice remained at duty until his battalion went out of the line.

There was another counter-attack on the evening of the 9th, accompanied by heavy shell-fire, during which, to everyone's regret, the Battalion Medical Officer, Captain Frere, was killed, and many other casualties were suffered.

On the night of the 10th/11th of June, the 6th Lincolns were relieved by the 34th Brigade and moved back to camp near Kemmel. The total casualties of the Battalion during the Battle of Messines 1917 were six officers and one hundred and sixty Other Ranks.

The Battalion remained in camp until the 18th of June, engaged in salvage work, and then began to march back in easy stages to Ganspette.

---

[8] 9514 Sgt. Riley Biggadike. Killed in action 07/06/1917, aged 22. He was the son of Elizabeth Biggadike, of East Lea Cottages, Holbeach, Lincolnshire and is commemorated on the Menin Gate, Belgium (panel 21).

# YPRES

*19 June 1917 – 10 October 1917*

Ganspette was a very charming place. Training was carried out but we didn't have to work too hard. A dispute with the Lancashire Fusiliers (34th Brigade) over a billet engaged most of our attention and time. The billet in question was a fine old château, situated on the boundary of the billeting area. Both Battalions desired it for their H.Q. we had occupied it and would not give it up. The Lancashire Fusiliers would never have known of it had not we, in mistaken kindness, allowed their Commanding Officer to live there with us. Having one room, this Commanding Officer wanted the whole place, and never rested until he had authority from Division to turn us out, when very resentfully, we went. A touch of humour was added to this incident by Captain Nightingale, the Adjutant of the Lancashire Fusiliers, who took a leading part in pressing their claims, being suddenly posted as Staff Captain to the 33rd Infantry Brigade, where he had to uphold our rights.

On July 1st the Battalion moved to Nortleulinghem, a village five miles away, situated right in the centre of the training area. Training became stiffer, consisting of Battalion and Brigade field days.

On July 13th the Battalion entrained at Watten and proceeded to Poperinghe, and thence to a camp hidden in a wood just off the Poperinghe - Ypres road, three miles from Ypres.

For some time past a big attack at Ypres had been contemplated, and preparations had been in progress for several months. The Messines-Wytschaete attack been only the first stop in the operations, for with the Messines Ridge in enemy hands, the whole salient was commanded by the enemy, the way was clear for the main attack east and north-east of Ypres.

The Commanding Officer, Lieut.-Colonel Gater D.S.O. rejoined from England the following day, re-assuming command of the Battalion, and on the 15th the Brigade moved into the line, the Battalion moving into Reserve on the Ypres Canal.

The artillery preparation, which in those days was extended over several weeks, had begun, and the enemy was replying very vigorously. The canal at this place ran through the cutting about 15' deep, and the eastern bank was honeycombed with shelters and dug-outs, which gave comparative security, except against direct hits. The enemy knew that a big concentration of men were kept in the canal cutting, and he was constantly shelling it. The shells would come skimming over, usually just clearing the eastern bank and bursting on the western side. Gas shells were being used very extensively by the enemy, and night after night we would have to wear our box respirators, often five hours on end.

A few casualties occurred: Captain Crick was slightly wounded, also Lieutenant Playle. On July 18th the Battalion relieved the Sherwood Foresters in the line, in the left sub-section of the Brigade front. 'A', 'C' and 'D' Companies took over the line, with 'B' Company in Reserve on the Canal Bank. The shelling on both sides was very heavy. Our artillery and trench mortars were busily engaged in wire cutting, and for the first time in our experience gas projectors were discharged on to the enemy lines. Patrols were sent out nightly to harass the enemy and prevent him from repairing his wire. A small raid was attempted but the enemy's trenches could not be entered, owing to our own artillery fire.

Inter-Company reliefs were carried out every two nights. On July 24th the 51st Division carried out a successful raid from our front, capturing four prisoners, and the same night were relieved by the 7th South Staffordshire Regiment and went back into Reserve on the Canal. The following day the Battalion again went into the line, this time in the right sub-sector, relieving the 6th Border Regiment. Shelling continued to be very heavy.

Our aeroplanes reported on July 27th that no sign of movement could be observed in the enemy forward positions, and it was thought by the Higher Command that the enemy, in anticipation of our attack, must have withdrawn, as they had done opposite the Guards Division further north the previous day. We were accordingly ordered to push out patrols immediately. Patrols were sent out, covered by the Battalion Scouts, under Sergeant Tapsell but they had hardly got through our own entanglements when a heavy rifle and machine fire was opened on them from a sap just opposite. Through his gallantry on this occasion, Sergeant Tapsell gained a bar to his Distinguished Conduct Medal[9]. Several casualties occurred, Lieutenant Playle, in charge of the patrol, was shot through the arm, and the patrols came back. The patrols of the 7th South Staffordshire on our left suffered much more severely.

The following night the Battalion was relieved by three battalions of the

---

[9] See Appendix II for Sgt. Tapsell's D.C.M. citations.

39th Division, and went back to camp in the wood. The fortnight in the line had been particularly trying. The Brigade had been holding the whole of the front on which the 51st and 39th Division were to attack a few days later. Casualties in the Battalion had been over a hundred and some battalions in the Brigade had suffered nearly twice that number. Early the next morning, when everyone, tired-out lay asleep in the wood, an enemy aeroplane flew over us and bombed us, causing twelve casualties. That was our first experience of bombs from aeroplanes, a branch of warfare then almost untried. We marched back to Saint Jans Ter Biezen on July 30th, a village three miles to the west of Poperinghe, and the next day the big attack started. The 51st and the 39th Divisions both made good progress but further south strong opposition was encountered and the advance was less satisfactory. Once more the weather favoured the enemy. On August 1st the rain began and lasted almost continuously for a week. In the driest weather the low lying country round Ypres is waterlogged. After any rain it becomes impassable.

On August 8th the battalion returned to the camp near Ypres and after staying there a week, moved up to Siege Camp, two miles from the Canal. Boche planes were over, bombing every night, and in area where every available yard was occupied by camps or horse lines, casualties were inevitable.

Our front line, on the 51st Division front, at this time ran along the Steenbeke, a small muddy stream running through the village of Saint Julien and west of Langemarck. On August 16th the 34th Brigade made an attack to capture the Pheasant Line, a trench situated on comparatively high ground, 1000 yards east of and parallel to the Steenbeke. This operation was only partly successful, the Pheasant Line being taken on the left, but on the right, owing to the next division not getting on, the 34th Brigade were unable to advance. Langemarck was taken.

The Battalion was ordered to supply two Companies as carrying parties for the 34th Brigade in this attack, 'A' and 'B' Companies being detailed. They did exceptionally fine work, carrying S.A.A.[10], water and rations right over the Steenbeke and into the front line within four hours after the attack had commenced.

On the right, where the attack had been held up, they came under heavy machine gun fire at close range; two casualties occurred. The next day, the Battalion moved up in support and two days later relieved the 7th South

---

[10] Small Arms Ammunition.

Staffords in the line between Langemarck and Saint Julien. The enemy resistance here was centred in concrete pill-boxes, which could hold anything up to a dozen men, were loop-holed on each side for machine guns, and were immune from anything but a direct hit from a very heavy shell. Many of them had been hit several times by 18-pdrs. 4.5", even 6" shells, but except for huge lumps of concrete being knocked off, they remained secure. To take these pillboxes was a problem. Their machine guns would fire right through an ordinary shrapnel barrage at our advancing infantry, and special tactics had to be devised to overcome them. A plan was eventually evolved by which small parties attacked the pillboxes from either flank, if possible getting in their 'blind spots', whilst a Lewis Gun engaged the front loopholes.

This method was successfully employed on August 22nd, when two Companies, 'B' and 'D', were ordered to attack and capture Bulow Farm, a large and strongly held pill box, situated among a group of smaller ones near the Pheasant Line. Captain Foster had been killed two nights before whilst on patrol, and 'D' Company was commanded by Captain Jones.[11] 'B' Company was still commanded by Captain Sutherland M.C. The attack was successful and Bulow Farm was taken with several prisoners. Captain Jones was killed during the attack and troops on the right again failing; our right flank had to be slightly withdrawn. Captain Sutherland M.C., did exceptionally fine work, for which he received the Distinguished Service Order. Lieutenant Denny and Second Lieutenants Wharrie and Robinson were wounded. Casualties numbered about fifty.

Relieved two days later, the Battalion went back again into Support, and after staying there five days, marched back to a camp west of Poperinghe. The succeeding days were spent in reorganising and training, and various games and sports. The weather was very fine and sunny, and the stay in this camp which we named Tay Camp, was very much enjoyed.

After staying at Tay Camp a short while, we moved still further back on September 11th to the Zutkerque area; there we found we had not yet finished with the Ypres fighting, and that our next task would be to take the village of Poelcapelle, situated a mile and a half behind the Pheasant Line, of which the 51st Division had by that time gained entire possession.

---

[11] Captain John Cecil Foster M.C. had unfortunately been killed by a sentry of the Gloucester Regiment on the morning of the August 21st. He is buried in Vlamertinghe New Military Cemetery Belgium.

Training for this operation began immediately, and special attention was paid to practising the approved method of overcoming pillboxes. Many were the changes of plans in those days, but it was finally decided that the 7th South Staffords and 9th Sherwood Foresters would carry out the attack, with the 6th Borders in Support and our own Battalion in Reserve.

About this time Brigadier-General Daly, who had commanded the Brigade for seven months, was appointed to command the 24th Division. His successor was Brigadier-General F.G. Spring D.S.O. of the Lincolnshire Regiment, who had been the Brigade-Major of the Brigade in England since its formation, and on Gallipoli.

Battalion and Brigade field days were held almost daily, under the eyes of the most exalted commanders and staff officers, who sometimes praised us and other times said we were wrong; a little bit of good. It was all part of the day's work however, and did not worry us. So long as our own General and Commanding Officer were satisfied, other opinions did not matter to us. The training continued until October 2nd, when the Brigade moved to Siege Camp. Better equipment was issued and two days later we moved into Reserve, once more on the Canal Bank.

The attack was delivered by the South Staffords and Sherwood Foresters, Poelcapelle was taken and the Battalion was not called upon, except for a sudden move to Gane Post in the old enemy support line, whence we returned to the canal bank six hours later.

The rain once more started and came down in torrents. We half expected on the night of the 4th/5th to be sent up to relieve the South Staffords and the Sherwood Foresters but they remained in the line until the following night, when the Brigade, with the exception of our own Battalion, was relieved by the 32nd Infantry Brigade. The other three battalions entrained. They had finished with the Ypres fighting but our troubles were not yet over.

It was decided that the 32nd Brigade should attack the positions which the enemy was holding on the eastern outskirts of Poelcapelle. The attack was delivered on October 8th, and the same day the Battalion moved up to the neighbourhood of Pheasant Line and Poelcapelle, in Reserve to the 32nd Brigade. Their attack failed, it was decided not to use our Battalion, and after two days in shell holes under heavy fire, we were relieved on the night of 10th/11th and entrained at Irish Farm.

# LENS AND HULLUCH

*11 October 1917 – 23 August 1918*

The Battalion detrained at Watten station, where buses were waiting, and returned to billets in Nortleulinghem, after an absence of nearly three months. We had just got comfortably settled down in Nortleulinghem, and had commenced training and re-organisation, when orders came that we were to move southwards to the Lens district. We entrained at Watten, on our way to the railway station, passing the Guards Division which was just coming back from the line, and the same night detrained at Lillers. We spent the night in billets close to Lillers and the following day did a march of fifteen miles to Noeux-les-Mines, in the centre of the mining district. The following evening we moved into Support, to replace the South Staffords, who were taking over the line. Our Transport Section and Quartermaster stores moved to Mazingarbe, a village near the Lens-Bethune road, four miles behind the line.

Then commenced a period of holding the line, which lasted nearly a year. The Canadians had been holding the line in front of Lens, and during the summer, with the 46th Division, had taken Hill 70, an important tactical feature east of Loos, which commanded the whole of the surrounding country, and had advanced our line into the outskirts of Lens itself. The 11th Division had relieved a Canadian Division which went to Ypres and took part in the Paschendale fighting.

On October 3rd we took over the line just north of Lens. The Boche were expecting a renewal of our attacks at Lens, and kept things fairly lively with minenwerfers[12]. The trenches had never been properly consolidated since they were taken and there was plenty of work to be done. Just after getting into the line we were unfortunate enough to have a ration party of eleven knocked out, and a few other casualties occurred. On October 30th we were relieved by the 9th West Yorks, and staying the night at Bully-Grenay, marched back to rest billets at Vaudricourt, two miles South of Bethune, then a flourishing town. The same day we received news that our Commanding Officer, Lieut.-Colonel G.W. Gater D.S.O., who had commanded us for over a year, had been appointed to command the 62nd Infantry Brigade. During the time he had been with us, by

---

[12] The German name for a class of short range mortars.

his energy, ability and bravery, and still more by his constant thought for the interests and comfort of his officers and men, the Colonel had endeared himself to every one of us. It was with many regrets that we said goodbye to him.

Lieut.-Colonel Bruce D.S.O. of the Glamorgan Yeomanry was appointed to take over command of the Battalion. No one was in the mood to welcome a stranger but it was not long before we all realised we had again been singularly fortunate in our Commanding Officer. Lieut.-Colonel Bruce remained with, and very ably commanded, the Battalion until the cessation of hostilities.

We remained at, Vaudricourt resting for a week, and then returned to the line in front of Lens, spending weeks alternately in the line and in Cite Saint Pierre in Support. The line began to get quieter, and life was more or less a routine. For six weeks we never came further back than Cite Saint Pierre, but in the cellars of this once prosperous and picturesque suburb we managed to be fairly comfortable. A canteen was established, a bath house fixed up and every effort was made to make the men as comfortable as possible.

Captain J.C.P. Howis M.C. was appointed Second in Command of the 1/4th Territorial Battalion of the Lincolnshire Regiment. Major S.J. Burnett had been classified unfit for further active service and so Major T.D. Sutherland D.S.O., M.C. was appointed Second in Command.

On December 22nd we were relieved by the 38th Canadian Battalion, and we arrived back in Vaudricourt the following day. Christmas was spent very merrily, and in the severe weather that followed, little work or training was possible. The Battalion Football Team began to show signs of brilliance and became the best team in the Division, which position it ever afterwards maintained.

A fair amount of range firing was carried out at Vaudricourt when the weather permitted. Many pleasant evenings were spent in Bethune, where there was an officers' club and other attractions. But at this time the Boche started bombing Bethune very heavily and it was unsafe to venture there after dark on a clear evening. Though only five miles from the line, Bethune had hardly been touched by shell fire and the inhabitants continued their normal occupations and mode of living. Indescribable havoc and destruction was caused by the bombing, and in a short time the town was nearly deserted.

At the neighbouring village of Verquin, concert parties frequently performed, and it was there we saw for the first time on January 2nd 1918, the First Army Concert Party.

*Fig. 10: Brigadier-General Sir Henry Gater, G.C.M.G., K.C.B., D.S.O & Bar (1919).*

On January 24th we marched to Mazingarbe, where we stayed four days in Support with two Companies in the trenches; then we took over the front line, in the right sub-section of the Brigade Front. The trenches were found to be in fairly good condition but repairs were constantly required, and we were kept busily engaged in this work. The Brigade was holding a section of the line opposite Hulluch. The artillery on both sides was quiet and casualties were very few.

The line in this district had changed very little since 1914. It ran through a rolling plain, once fertile arable land, now mown over everywhere with grass.

By successive attacks in 1915, 1916 and 1917, the enemy had been pressed back until the line ran just in front of the ruins of Hulluch. Foss S.K. (held by the enemy), a mile and a half to the North, commanded the whole of the plain, as did from the South, Hill 70, which was in our hands. Three miles behind the enemy trenches could be seen the Wingles Towers, giving splendid observation to the enemy.

Screens had been constructed at intervals right across the plain to give cover from these towers. Behind our own positions rose the Philosophe Fosse, commanding the Rutoire Plain, which extended from our trenches to Philosophe. Philosophe, once a mining village, still contained a few inhabitants and the mine was worked when visibility was bad. West of Philosophe was the village of Mazingarbe, at that time quite intact, whilst to the North at Vermelles, in ruins, its chief landmark was the water tower - a favourite ranging mark for the enemy guns and a spot to be avoided. The sub-soil everywhere was chalk, and many deep dug-outs had been constructed, and in addition, a system of long tunnels, usually connecting the reserve lines with the front line.

Time passed fairly quickly, the Battalion doing a turn in the Front Line, then in the Support Trenches, and going back for a short rest, after which the performance was repeated. Early in February, the 6th Border Regiment was disbanded, and with only three battalions in the Brigade, we had more time in the line and less in Mazingarbe. A feature of life in this sector of the line was the frequency of our gas discharge, usually by means of projectors, once from cylinders, and later by gas beams. The cylinder discharge was not a great success. For a month we waited patiently for a favourable wind, with the cylinders in position in our trenches. In the meantime the enemy became aware of them and our trenches came in for heavy shelling and trench mortar bombardments, intended to destroy the cylinders. Little damage was done to them however, and finally they were discharged.

In the middle of March things began to get more lively. The enemy started to shell systematically our forward positions; the guns in Rutoire Plain, and also the villages of Mazingarbe and Philosophe. Noeux-les-Mines, six miles back, also received considerable attention from a High Velocity Gun. We afterwards discovered it was a feint to cover the enemy's preparations for his big offensive on the Somme. Once the latter had commenced, things speedily became normal again on our front.

In connection with the enemy's offensive down South, and in view of the possibility of an attack on our own front, identifications of the opposing forces were urgently required. A raid was accordingly planned and 160 men from 'C' and 'D' Companies under Major Sutherland D.S.O. M.C., Captain Bone of 'C' Company and Captain Shephard of 'D' Company commenced to train at Mazingarbe.

The place selected for the raid was 1500 yards south of Hulluch, where the enemy's front, support and second support lines formed a lozenge shaped figure.

The raid was carried out with an artillery, machine gun and trench mortar barrage on the morning of April 2nd at 8 a.m. It was a misty morning, which effectively hid our preparations, and the raid came as a complete surprise to the enemy.

'D' Company, under Captain Shephard and Lieutenant Pattinson entered the first and second line, and 'C' Company under Captain Bone and Second Lieutenant Malkinson entered the third line, where two trench mortars and many dugouts were blown up with mobile charges. Machine guns coming into action on the flanks were disposed of. The raid was carried out without a hitch. Except in the third line, little opposition was encountered and the artillery, machine gun and smoke barrage stopped any interference from the enemy reserve trench or from the flanks.

One officer and thirty men were captured, and in addition many casualties were inflicted. One machine gun was brought in and several others which had been taken could not be brought back. Our own casualties were four men killed, two missing and fifteen wounded. There were no officer casualties.

The next occurrence of importance was the enemy attack between Givenchy and Armentières in April. We were then three or four miles South of La Bassée Canal, the southern limit of the enemy attack. For several days previously the enemy shelled continuously with gas shells our forward positions and particularly our batteries. Box respirators were worn for hours on end until, from sheer exhaustion; men were compelled to take them off. Casualties were fairly heavy, though very few fatalities occurred. For several days communications with the front line from Brigade H.Q. at Mazingarbe was very difficult, owing to a belt of gas which persisted for some time on Rutoire Plain.

Then, one very misty morning, we heard heavy firing to the north, not very far away, and more shells descended on us. Towards midday, we heard that there had been a raid on the 55th Division at Givenchy, and it later transpired that this raid had been an attack on a twenty mile front. The gas shelling was obviously to put our guns out of action and prevent them from harassing the enemy's flank and communications.

After that we were expecting the attack daily to extend South of La Bassée Canal, for by driving us back only a mile or two, the enemy could have stopped the Noeux-les-Mines coal miners from working. Nowhere else along the whole front would a short advance on the part of the enemy be of such tactical advantage to him, and we were flattered to think, or be told that, we were holding the most important part of the line.

From prisoners' statements it appeared that on several occasions the enemy was about to attack on our front but in each case plans were altered at the last moment. We were told that the Boche realised how strong we had made our positions, and could not risk an attack; but I am afraid we regarded this statement only as inducement to continue digging trenches.

Eventually, the attack up north having been held, things once more became normal, and on May 2nd the Brigade was relieved by the 34th Brigade after 99 days in the line. We went back to a camp in Froissart Wood, near Hersin but still within range of the Boche guns. After eight days resting and training there, the Brigade relieved the 32nd Infantry Brigade, this time in the Saint Eloi Section. We relieved the 6th Yorkshire Regiment in Support at Vermelles.

Then followed a period during which the Division had two Brigades in the line and one out resting. The sixteen days spent in the line would be alternately in the Hulluch and Saint Eloi Sections, and our period of rest at Mazingarbe, Noeux-les-Mines and Hersin. This system of relief was naturally a great improvement on the previous one, under which we were always in the line or in support, and never got further back than Mazingarbe. Life became a routine and with few exceptions, nothing of importance occurred. One of these exceptions was a gas projector discharge by the enemy at the end of May, with our own gas projectors captured on the Somme. We were in the right sub-section of the Saint Eloi Section at the time. A wiring party was caught and several casualties occurred, most of them unfortunately proved fatal. Second Lieutenant

Lockyear, our intelligence Officer, who was out putting up notice boards, was severely wounded by a projector burst, and was gassed so badly that he died a few hours later. Second Lieutenant Pocklington did several exciting patrols, during one of which he was wounded. Captain Fenwick, Commanding 'A' Company, who joined the Battalion on its formation in England, was killed whilst on patrol.

Whilst having our periodic rests we did very interesting field days on the Lorette Ridge, co-operating with tanks. But we began to get very fed up with life in the trenches, after so many months of it. Everything was so automatic and so much a matter of routine that we began to forget almost that the war still continued and certainly there was a great danger of losing one's self-reliance.

On August 23rd, whilst in support at Vermelles, we were relieved by the 6th Cameron Highlanders, and entrained on a light railway at Bully-Grenay; we moved back to La Thieuloye, a few miles north east of Saint Pol.

# FINAL OPERATIONS

*24 August 1918 – 30 June 1919*

At La Thieuloye we commenced training, eager for the opportunity of moving warfare once more. We expected to have a fortnight in which to prepare but our expectations were not realised. Orders were received to be ready to move at short notice, and on August 29th we moved by bus to Ecurie, three miles north of Arras, where we stayed the night in huts. The following day the Battalion marched to Grange Hill, south of Fouchy on the River Scarpe, and after a short rest took over the line at Boiry-Notre-Dame, seven miles east of Arras.

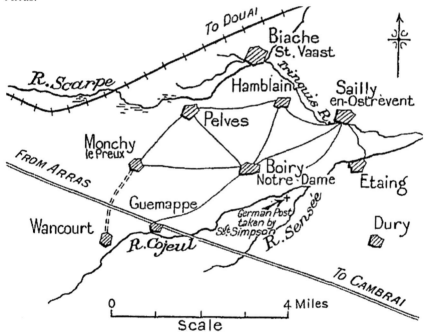

*Fig. 11: The Second Battle of Arras, 1918.*

A short time before, the Canadians, co-operating with an attack further south, had captured Monchy-le-Preux, which had been in enemy hands since the retirement in the spring, and had pushed on as far as Boiry-Notre-Dame. At the same time, the 51st Division, attacking north of the Scarpe, had captured Gavrelle and Plouvain. Such was the situation when we took over the line. Our front line ran roughly north-south, a mile east of Boiry. By sending out daylight patrols we discovered that the enemy was not holding the high ground east of the Sailly-Etaing road, so our posts were pushed forward to seize it.

On September 2nd the Canadians, South of the Cojeul River on our right, delivered a heavy attack on the Drocourt-Quéant Line, part of the Hindenburg Line, and pierced it completely, capturing the villages of Dury and Lécluse, and other village further south. This attack partially cut off the village of Etaing on our right front. To harass the enemy troops in this village, a fighting patrol under Lieutenant Barrett was sent out. Sergeant Evans, who was with the patrol, located an enemy post on the south bank of the Cojeul River, and swimming across, single-handed he attacked the post, shot the two sentries with his revolver, and captured the remaining four men of the post. The patrol then crossed higher up by a bridge and soon after, coming under very heavy fire, Second Lieutenant Barrett was severely wounded and one man was killed. With great gallantry, Sergeant Evans got the wounded officer back, having to go into the stream to do so, as the Boche kept up a heavy rifle and machine-gun fire. For his bravery Sergeant Evans was awarded the Victoria Cross.[13]

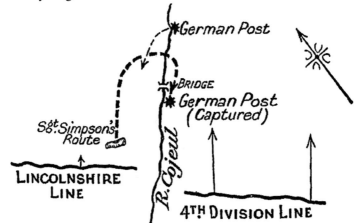

*Fig. 12: Sergeant Evans wins the V.C.*

---

[13] The award of the Victoria Cross to Sergeant Evans was announced in the London Gazette on 31st March 1919 and presented to him by the King on 05/12/1918. The citation was originally published under his alias, Walter Simpson, but this was later amended to his real name - Arthur Evans. The official citation is provided in Appendix II.

The following day the 4th Division on our right entered Etaing, the enemy having cleared out during the night. The ground between Sailly and Etaing was very low and marshy, and was gradually being submerged by the rising waters. Somewhere near Biache-Saint-Vaast the Boche had dug a channel connecting the Scarpe and Trinquise Rivers, and the Scarpe, being above the level of the low-lying ground in the Trinquise Valley, much of the latter was flooded.

On September 7th the Brigade was relieved by the 32nd Infantry Brigade and we went back to reserve in trenches near Monchy. Four days later we returned to the line, this time in the Hamblain-les-Prés subsection, with our northern boundary the River Scarpe. The shelling was at times fairly heavy, and the Divisional Commander was wounded whilst walking round our front. In the line until September 15th, we were relieved by the South Staffords, and went back into support at Monchy-le-Preux.

Enemy aeroplanes were continually attacking and bringing down our observation balloons. This became so regular an occurrence that we used to have all the Lewis Guns in the Battalion – thirty-six of them – mounted ready for the coming of the enemy aeroplane, which would suddenly come into sight, diving steeply at the balloon from a cloud. The two observers in the balloon would jump out and come sailing down in their parachutes. Archie would blaze away and there would be a terrific rattle of Lewis Gun fire. But we never hit anything unless it was the balloon. The enemy aeroplane would fire a short burst of tracer bullets at the balloon, turn sharply round and make off, whilst the balloon would slowly burst into flames and fall gently to the earth. The two observers always fell near our mess, and we got so much into the habit of expecting them, that at 4 p.m. each day, the time they usually came down, we would get two stiff whiskies. The same two officers were brought down five times in seven days.

On September 19th the Division was relieved by the 4th Division and we went back by bus to La Thieuloye. Again, we were there only a short time, during which little training was possible, and on September 25th we were once more in buses returning to the line. Later at night we debussed at Vis-en-Artois, on the Arras - Cambrai road, and marched to Choisy, where we slept in any shelter we could find. The next day saw us in the Drocourt-Quéant Line, taken by the Canadians three weeks previously, and there we moved up to the Buissy Switch on September 27th, the morning the Canadian Corps had attacked the enemy's lines on the Canal du Nord.

Crossing the Canal at Marquion they captured Bourlon Wood and the village of Bourlon. The 32nd and 34th Infantry Brigades of our own Division, crossing the Canal four hours after Zero, swung northwards and captured Sauchy-Lestrée. The 34th Infantry Brigade continued their advance northwards and took the village of Oisy-le-Verger; whilst the 32nd Infantry Brigade secured Epinoy, three miles east of the Canal.

From the Buissy Switch we saw the whole of this attack, to which we were in Reserve. Everywhere the attacking troops were completely successful, and to our disappointment we were not called on.

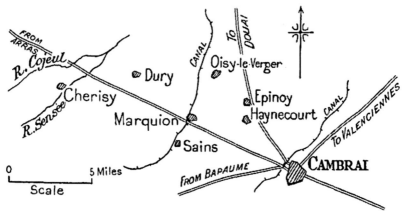

*Fig. 13: Map of the Marquion area.*

The following day the Canadians continued to advance towards Cambrai. We crossed the Canal to trenches between Marquion and Sauchy-Lestrée but two days later we returned to the Buissy Switch. On October 1st the whole Brigade crossed the canal to the Marquion area. The following day the Brigade relieved the 2nd Canadian Infantry Brigade in the line and we moved into support near the Arras-Cambrai Road, two miles east of Marquion. We took over the line from the 34th Brigade, with our front line on the railway, south of Aubencheul-au-Bac. Here the enemy held a narrow strip of ground a mile in width on the South side of the Sensée Canal. His line of resistance was the railway, here running roughly east-west, and it was protected by strong belts of uncut barbed wire. We forthwith made arrangements to attack the enemy's position, capture Aubencheul and occupy the south bank of the Sensée Canal. Arrangements were made for tanks to assist us by making gaps through the wire.

During the night of October 6th/7th information was received from 56th Division on our left that their patrols, operating towards Aubencheul from the

South West had met with no opposition. 'C' Company, under Captain Crick, was ordered to attack Aubencheul immediately, and 'A' Company under Captain Tolley was ordered to clear the enemy's positions on the railway line, and get in touch with the 7th South Staffords on the right, who were advancing to the railway.

Both these operations were carried out with complete success. 'C' Company advancing in small parties surprised the remaining enemy posts in Aubencheul; Sergeant Evans again distinguishing himself in rushing a post, and gaining the Distinguished Conduct Medal. The south bank of the canal was occupied but the bridge of Aubencheul was found to have been blown up. The enemy had to retain touch with the south bank by means of a footbridge east of Aubencheul. Meanwhile, 'A' Company had successfully occupied the railway line. A patrol under Captain Tolley, working east along the railway, inflicted heavy casualties on a large enemy post they encountered. Both Captain Crick and Captain Tolley were awarded the Military Cross for their work that night.

On October 9th information was received that the enemy was retiring. The Battalion was hurriedly relieved by the London Scottish, 56th Division, and advanced about three and a half miles to a position between Abancourt and the village of Hem-Lenglet on the Sensée Canal.

In the meantime we heard that Cambrai had been entered by the Canadians. The following day, a daylight patrol under Second Lieutenant Blackham, pushed on under heavy machine gun fire to the outskirts of Hem-Lenglet, where it held on till nightfall, when 'B' Company attacked and captured Hem-Lenglet. Thirteen prisoners, including one wounded officer, were taken; a large number of the enemy were killed, and five machine guns were captured. Our casualties were light. Second Lieutenant Cowan was wounded and Captain Shephard, Lieutenant Horry and Second Lieutenant Horsburgh had been wounded before the attack commenced. The Canal bank was occupied.

Two days later the Battalion was relieved by the 26th Canadians and moved back to dugouts and bivouacs on the Arras-Cambrai road between Raillencourt and Marquion. The Battalion remained there, resting and training until October 19th when we marched to Escaudoeuvres, north east of Cambrai. Two days later we moved forward two miles to Naves, and thence to Villers-en-Cauchies, where training was resumed.

The enemy was now in rapid retirement all along the line but at the same time was fighting a stubborn rearguard action. In his retirement he systematically mined and blew up crossroads, destroyed railways, blew up bridges and put every possible obstacle in the way of our advance.

On November 1st the Battalion received orders to proceed to Verchain with a view to relieving a battalion of the 4th Division, then in the line. This move was completed during the afternoon and we went into billets in Verchain for the night.

The following day the Brigade relieved the 10th Infantry Brigade in the line, and we were in Support with 'A' and 'C' Companies in close support to the Sherwood Foresters in front of Artres. The remaining two companies and Battalion H.Q. were in a railway cutting between Artres and Querenaing.

On November 3rd the Battalion moved forward in support to the Sherwood Foresters, whose role was to attack at Curgies, and obtained possession of the railway line and high ground beyond. This operation was successfully carried out.

The next day the Battalion was again in support to the Sherwood Foresters, who were ordered to force the crossings of the Aunelle River at Sebourg. The Sherwood Foresters met with stubborn resistance whilst effecting the crossing but succeeded in doing so. Their attack on the high ground beyond, however, failed owing to the intensity of the machine gun fire, which the enemy brought to bear from the crest of the ridge and from the flanks.

Advancing again on the 5th under an artillery barrage, the Sherwood Foresters captured the high ground, meeting with little resistance. We were then ordered to pass through the Sherwood Foresters and occupy the high ground between Roisin and Angreau. This was done. The enemy shelled the whole area heavily during the afternoon and evening, putting down occasional barrages on Angreau and the Angreau River. 'A' and 'C' Companies were sent forward to occupy the ridge east of the Angreau River but were unable to obtain the crest until nightfall, owing to the heavy machine gun fire from Angre Wood. Rain had fallen all day and all night, and the ground was a morass.

On the 6th we were ordered to advance again. Two Companies 'A' and 'C' were ordered to force the crossings of the Grande Honnelle and capture the railway line in Angre Wood, whilst 'B' Company was ordered to force the crossing before Autreppe, with 'D' Company in support. The attack went forward under a barrage but was held up at the river by the violent machine gun fire.

The enemy were holding the railway embankment in strength and were little affected by the barrage, having cut holes in the rear face of the embankment where they took cover until the barrage was past. A few men of

'A' and 'C' Companies under Second Lieutenant Wilson got across the river but were unable to hold on, as they were enfiladed from both flanks, and as they began to climb the embankment, they were bombed by the enemy. Severe casualties were sustained here, and Second Lieutenant Wilson was missing. 'B' Company was also held up.

The following day the Battalion was ordered to repeat the attack on the crossings before Autreppe. After this had been effected, one Company was to push forward to the line of the Montignies-Bavay Road, and establish itself thus facing east, whilst 'C' Company in support was to form a defensive flank to the North.

The attack met with little opposition, 'B' Company crossed the river and pushed out to the road. 'D' Company cleared the village and 'A' Company formed a defensive flank, whilst 'C' Company were in reserve. The objective was taken, and positions were consolidated by 2 p.m. as the Bois Daubois was still occupied by enemy machine guns, and formed a good assembly position for an enemy counter-attack, it was decided to clear it. The forward batteries of 18-pdrs and 4.5" howitzers put an extensive bombardment on it from 4.30 p.m. to 4.50 p.m., and then two platoons went through it, clearing it of the enemy, and establishing posts on the further side. The enemy shelled Autreppe and the river crossings very heavily up till 6 p.m. when his shelling ceased and the night was quiet. Casualties were slight.

During the operations, Major Sutherland D.S.O. M.C., did excellent work in directing the attacking Companies for which he was awarded a bar to his Distinguished Service Order.

The Battalion remained in billets at Autreppe and also the following day. On the 9th the advance was resumed. The South Staffords and Sherwood Foresters passed through to the Mons-Maubeuge road, and the Battalion was in Brigade Reserve, having fought its last fight. We proceeded to billets in Aulnois, arriving there after a very long and tiring march over roads badly cut up and filled with heavy traffic. The next day the Battalion moved to billets in L'Ermitage.

During the morning of the November 11th, 1918, the Battalion was marching to Quévy-le-Grand, when news was received that the Armistice had been signed and that hostilities would cease at 11.00 a.m. that morning. A cheer was raised by the leading section of fours and passed right down the column. That was all! Everyone was too weary and exhausted at the time to show much emotion.

We arrived at Quévy-le-Grand and got settled into our billets; and the day which meant so much, which we had dreamed of for long years in Gallipoli, on the desert, in the muddy trenches of France, had come. Many had been the plans made for its celebration. When existence had seemed unbearable, we had consoled ourselves by picturing what we would do on the day the fighting stopped. And what did we do now that the eventful day had arrived? Nothing! We were too tired to think of anything but rest, and we had neither beer nor whisky. Little remained to be told. From Quévy-le-Grand we marched back to Presnes, a village between Conde and Valenciennes, and there demobilisation started.

It was not the end we had pictured. We had always hoped to return home as a Battalion, all to be disbanded together. Instead of which, officers and men slipped away day by day until few remained. And we who are left think of the times which have been; of the many friends we have in the Battalion, whose lives henceforward lie apart from us, and of the many friends who will never be demobilised and return home, whose last resting place is the battlefield where they have fallen.

# POSTSCRIPT I

## THE TAKING OF CHOCOLATE HILL
### 7 August 1915

<u>Editor's Note:</u>  Colonel F.G. Spring wrote the following postscript in response to a copy of the official draft of the Suvla Landing and sent it to Brigadier-General C.F. Aspinall-Oglander C.B. C.M.G. D.S.O. who was responsible for compiling the British Official History of the Military Operations in Gallipoli.

I hope you will give the Lincolns and Borders more credit for what they did. The capture of Chocolate Hill was entirely due to them and in no way to the Irish Battalions, who weren't for the job and never attempted to get on, even when the Lincolns passed through them.  See what Norton, a Company Commander of 6th Lincolns says in a letter he wrote last year to General Maxwell (with reference to some remarks in a draft of the 11th Division History), which you will find at the end of my history.

You have quite rightly criticised the 32nd and 34th Brigades of 11th Division for not getting on earlier in the day, but when you come to the 31st Brigade (five battalions) of 10th Division, you try to excuse them by saying that they were checked by shrapnel fire, and simply had not been trained for open warfare.  Why should they be excused when this same fire did not stop the Lincolns and Borders in their advance?

The impression you give on page 26 is that the Lincolns and Borders carried the Irish battalions along with them on to Chocolate Hill.  This is quite wrong.  The Irish Battalions made no attempt to go on with the Lincolns and Borders (except one officer and a few men of the Royal Dublin Fusiliers): they definitely failed and the taking of Chocolate Hill was done entirely by the Lincolns and Borders.  The draft as written gives quite an inaccurate impression.

You will see in Hansen's account of Chocolate Hill on page 106 that the Royal Dublin Fusiliers came up after the Lincolns had taken the Hill[14]. I know it was some considerable time after Hansen had phoned back to me to say that the Hill was taken before any of the 31st Brigade reported back that they were on the Hill.

It was really a fine performance of the Lincolns and Borders, and I am sure

---

[14] Hansen's account is provided in Postscript III.

that they could have done it earlier in the day as you suggest on page 24. The ten days at Helles under service conditions had made all the difference to the Brigade; they went in raw and came out soldiers.

You can get first hand information about this attack from the following officers of the 6th Lincolns, who were in it:

Lieut.-Colonel A.E. NORTON D.S.O. (Company Commander)
       'Scrivens'
        Chiltern Candover
        Alresford, Hants.

Lieut.-Colonel A.C. CROYDON M.C., D.C.M. (Company Commander)
        Haberdashers Hall
        Gresham Street
        London E.C.

Major P.H. HANSEN V.C., D.S.O., M.C. (Adjutant)
        2nd Bn. The Lincolnshire Regiment
        Dover.

I do not understand why Sitwell did not report the capture till 1 a.m. After going with the Lincolns at the start across the Salt Lake, I returned to our Brigade H.Q. near the Cut, close to Sitwell's Brigade H.Q. and was in touch with each battalion by a telephone, which the Lincolns ran out behind them.

As soon as the Lincolns reported capture of Chocolate Hill I repeated it verbally to General Maxwell and General Sitwell - some considerable time after the Lincolns had reported this, a Company Liaison Officer of some battalion of 31st Brigade rang up to say he was the senior officer on the Hill and asked to speak to General Hill! After this Sitwell told Hill he had better go and take over Chocolate Hill and get the Battalions re-organised. I went over later with a string of men carrying ammunition and stretcher bearers, and found the Lincolns and Borders quite happy and expecting to be ordered to push on to 'W' Hill at dawn. I met General Hill before dawn and he said he would not want the Lincolns and Borders any longer and they could go away, so I telephoned back to General Maxwell at Brigade H.Q., who reported to Divisional H.Q. and we got orders to return to Lala Baba as Divisional Reserve, which we did just after dawn. This was a mistake, as otherwise these two battalions could have been on 'W' Hill early on the morning of 8th August. Whether they sent out scouts or not after taking Chocolate Hill I don't know but Hansen could tell you.

Does this not all go to prove the risk of employing troops who have never been in action before, on an operation of this kind? If all the 11th Division had had ten days in the line at Helles I believe the 32nd and 34th Brigades would have taken their objective.

## 8th August
The lack of drive on this day was ruinous to any chances we had of getting on. I remember during the morning sitting at Lala Baba with General Maxwell trying to see what was happening - absolute peace reigned and not a shot was going off; it was dreadful to see it.

## 9th August
See Hansen's notebook,[15] which will give you much information about action of 9th August.

The 6th Dublins were later ordered to move in support of the centre of the three attacking battalions.

As you say on page 7, General Maxwell had seen on the afternoon of 8th August that a Battalion of the 32nd Brigade was in Scimitar Hill (Hill 70), and made his plans accordingly.

This Battalion was withdrawn by 32nd Brigade during the night and we were not informed of this - hence the box up when deploying in the morning, when it was found the Turks were there.

## Artillery Support
We had one Field Battery supporting us; the Major was wounded at the start and shortly after the only other Regular Officer (a Second Lieutenant). The Mountain Guns did their best but could not reach the Turks with whom the Lincolns were engaged - from our Brigade H.Q. on Lala Baba we could see the Lincolns and the Turks.

\*\*\*\*\*

I was wounded in the morning of 9th August so cannot say anything about

---

[15] See Postscript III.

subsequent operations, but in my history you will see notes up to 21st August from letters I received.  An account I wrote out for General Maxwell a few years ago as to what I saw on 8th and 9th August, which you will find at the end of the Appendices in my history, will give you some local colouring.[16]

F.G. SPRING, Col.
Long Hedge
Salisbury
26th Jan. 1931

---

[16] This account is provided in Postscript II.

# POSTSCRIPT II

*NOTES ON SUVLA LANDING*
*6 – 7 August 1915*

Editor's Note: The following postscript was written by Colonel F.G. Spring to Brigadier-General R.P. Maxwell, with reference to a draft of the 11th Division History. These remarks were subsequently sent to Brigadier-General C.F. Aspinall-Oglander C.B. C.M.G. D.S.O. and put on record for the official draft of the Suvla Landing.

I've often wondered what were the feelings of the men sitting crowded up in the bottom decks on this hot night, possibly feeling sea-sick! Added to this, none of the 11th Division, except 33rd Infantry Brigade had been under fire. I imagine the state of mind of a man who had been, say, a clerk in civil life, going through all these hours with the thought of a battle on landing in a strange country.

I've always understood, and heard it at the time, that in the night the 32nd and 34th Brigades fired into one another, and small wonder when the 34th were landed by the Navy 1000 yards south of where they should have been. This mistake of the Navy seems to have been the primary cause of the trouble and delay in the early morning of 7th August. Wright, who commanded the Manchesters, told me that the first man of his battalion was drowned in stepping off the lighter.

## Re: Two Battalions of 33rd Brigade sitting idle on Lala Baba

As written, this gives the impression that General Maxwell should have taken action, which he could not have done. Firstly, these two battalions were in <u>Divisional Reserve</u> and the 32nd Brigade was in front of them. Secondly, if I give you a short account of what happened to the 33rd Brigade after landing till dawn on 7th August, you will see they could not have been used. The two leading battalions after landing (South Staffords and Sherwood Foresters) went off to hold from Salt Lake to the sea. These two battalions then came directly under Divisional H.Q. and not under General Maxwell.

As 33rd Brigade H.Q., 6th Lincolns and Borders were forming up after landing, I went off to get in touch with 32nd Brigade, who had moved off. I went towards Lala Baba and luckily came across the G.S.O.1. (Lieut.-Colonel Malcolm), who told me that the Divisional H.Q., after landing, found themselves in the midst of a fight. He then told me we should move by the east of Lala Baba and along west side of Salt Lake to our rendezvous, vis-à-vis the junction of Anafarta Road and Razmak Ravine. I went back and told General Maxwell, and we started off at the head of the two battalions. The going was awful and eventually each battalion was strung out to a great length. As it was getting light, the head of the Lincolns, where we were, was approaching the Cut and we could see fighting going on ahead by the rifle flashes. As soon as it got light the Turks started firing into us and so General Maxwell halted the Lincolns on the isthmus between Lala Baba and the Cut, and the Borders on Lala Baba, their head had only got to Lala Baba. You will see what he says in his notes at the end of the history I wrote. I don't see what else he could have done, and being strung out we certainly could not have been used before dawn.

Surely the 32nd Brigade were beyond the Cut by this time (5 a.m.). I think it should have been made clear that 33rd Brigade (less two battalions) was in Divisional Reserve.

Colonel Daukes, 7th Staffords, who was in command of 7th Staffords and 9th Sherwood Foresters, reported direct to Divisional H.Q. These two battalions since landing had been taken away from General Maxwell.

We were longer than a week at Helles. We landed on night 19/20th July, were attached to the Naval Division, and took over the whole of their front on nights 20th/21st or 21st/22nd July, being relieved on night 1st/2nd August.

# POSTSCRIPT III

*6TH BATTALION OPERATIONAL REPORT*
*7 – 9 August 1915*

Editor's Note: The following text is a transcription of a handwritten report made by Captain Hansen V.C. for the operations of the 7th-9th August 1915. This account appears as an appendix to the 33rd Infantry Brigade War Diary, and is now held by The National Archives (WO 95/4299 parts 47-48).

## Report on Action of August 7th

On August 7th the Battalion was in Divisional Reserve. At 2 p.m. orders were received to advance in support of 31st Brigade who had landed earlier in the day and were to attack Yilghin Burnu on Chocolate Hill. We were supported by the Border Regiment. 'C' and 'D' Companies started off supported by 'A' and 'B'. We advanced to a point north of Salt Lake where the order was received that we were to attack the Hill as the troops ordered to do so had not yet moved. The Battalion speedily came under heavy shrapnel fire but advanced in extended order across the open without flinching. About 200 yards from the foot of the Hill the Battalion halted under cover with the supports of the Royal Dublin Fusiliers. 'D' and 'B' Companies then advanced through the Royal Dublin Fusiliers in short rushes. Major Norton was hit and Captain Duck took command of 'D' Company. Companies where then more or less split up owing to casualties and to small sections of the Royal Dublin Fusiliers who were lying behind cover.

Companies were therefore reorganised and 'B' and 'D' companies prepared for the assault, proceeding up the Hill under more or less heavy rifle fire. About 100 yards from the top of the hill a last halt was made in dead ground. This lasted half an hour owing to our own artillery and machine guns playing on the top of the hill. The charge then took place and the enemy were dispersed, many being killed and wounded and all who were able to get away retiring by a communication trench on the far side of the hill.

Captain Duck and Lieutenant Webber were the first to go over the enemy fire trench. Unfortunately Lieutenant Webber got shot under the heart while actually crossing the fire trench and fell into it. He must have been shot by a wounded Turk.

Shortly after, the Royal Dublin Fusiliers came up and preparations were then made for the counter-attack.

The losses in this fight were five Officers and 164 Rank and File. Major D'A.M. Fraser and Lieutenant Webber were killed. Second Lieutenants Bird and Hemsley and Major Norton being wounded.

This was our first success and I feel proud of the great achievement of the Battalion.

## Report on Action of August 9th

The Battalion left bivouacs at 2 a.m. and proceeding by the north of the Salt Lake watched the points of development at 4.10 a.m., and immediately deployed into two lines of half battalions on a front of 500 yards. Our objective was the high ridge south-west of Anafarta Sagir on which we were ordered to entrench.

The attack was led by 'A' Company on the right supported by 'D' and 'B' Company on the left supported by 'C'. After a short halt to enable the South Staffordshire Regiment to come up on our right, the attack went on. The Commanding Officer was then informed that we were 100 yards too much to the right. This was soon corrected and the attack proceeded on a knoll known as Hill 90.

To continue in the Commanding Officer's words:

*The Battalion reached this point which I had been told was held by one of our Regiments (the West Yorkshires) which information I had passed on to [my] Company Commanders. When firing started, I immediately went to the leading companies who pushed on, taking up a position along the forward head of the Hill (see sketch). I then heard that the West Yorkshires had retired from the hill and 'D' Company was forced to turn half left to meet an attack from the enemy on the flank. Casualties began at once. I went to 'D' where I found the line held but under a very accurate and close, if not heavy fire, both from the front of 'B' and the high ground beyond. I then went to the left flank (near 'IX') where the men were quite steady and shooting hard. There were many casualties from fire from 'A' and the high ground beyond it. I then fixed on a central point as Battalion Headquarters. I and my Adjutant were there at intervals during the entire action and sent messages from there. A few reinforcements now began to arrive but in small numbers, a company or less at a time, and went up into the firing line. I then sent a report to Headquarters asking for more reinforcements and ammunition. I then went to 'X', where I found Major Yool of the South Staffordshire Regiment. The bushes were full of dead and wounded and I believe this corner was hardly held all day as no one could get through the bush. As I returned there was a rush of men to the rear – composed of Territorials – which I, helped by Captain Hansen and Captain Duck managed to stop, sending all the men back to the firing line. There were several of these rushes (seven or eight), two at 'B' all of which we managed to stop, taking the men back to the firing line. All the time shrapnel was bursting among the men from the right front. These added to the casualties.*

*Fire came directly from the rear and pitched amongst the men. There is no doubt that these came from our own guns.*

*During this time three small fires had started at '1X' and '2X' but they had gone out. A further fire started now, however, and got a good hold of the scrub, driving back the men in the firing line and making it almost impossible to see. Unfortunately there were very much too many wounded to bring away. At 12.15 p.m. I reluctantly gave the order to withdraw, taking as many wounded as we could. There were then only twenty-three men left on the Hill – mostly men of the Battalion.*

*I retired on a trench about three hundred yards in the rear and took over a section of the defence, which we immediately consolidated.*

Our losses were:
12 Officers and 391 Rank and File killed, wounded and missing; out of 17 Officers, 561 Rank and File who originally started out; leaving the Battalion: 5 Officers, 174 Rank and File strong.

The Officers wounded:

Killed:         Captain P.L. Browne
                  Lieut. T.G. Parkin
                  Lieut. G.M. Hewart

Wounded:       Major W.E.W. Elkington
                    Captain A.C. Croydon
                    Lieut. G.C. Downes
                    Lieut. K.J.W. Peake
                    Lieut. C.H.A French
                    2/Lieut. R.D. Foster
                    2/Lieut. R.L. Hornsby

Wounded and missing believe killed:
                    Captain J.T. Lewis

Missing:        Lieut. R.L. Cook

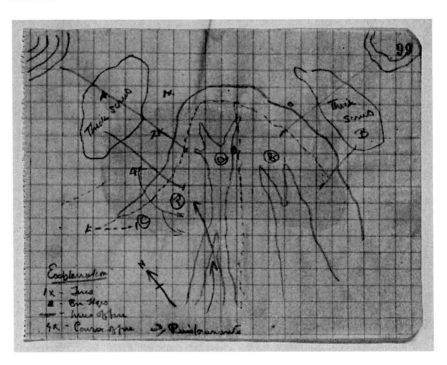

*Fig. 14: Sketch map by Captain Hansen V.C.*

# POSTSCRIPT IV

*CAPTAIN CROYDON'S ACCOUNT*
*6 – 9 August 1915*

<u>Editor's Note:</u> The following report was written retrospectively by Lt.-Colonel A.C. Croydon M.C., D.C.M. and describes his experiences during the Lincolns attack on Chocolate Hill and Anafarta Ridge, as commander of 'A' Company. This account was put also on record for the official draft of the Suvla Landing and is now held at The National Archives (CAB 45/228).

## The Suvla Landing: August 6th-7th

We landed during the night from destroyers and flat-bottomed boats and next morning found ourselves near the Hill "Lala Baba"

On the afternoon of the 7th, my battalion received orders to support the 10th Division in the attack on "Chocolate Hill". 'A' and 'C' Companies under Major Fraser being on the right, and 'B' and 'D' Companies under Major Norton, on the left. We then went forward in artillery formation from Lala Baba and when clear of the Hill, 'A' and 'C' Companies deployed to the right across the Salt Lake, and then opened out in extended order – 'C' Company on the right and 'A' Company on the left. We advanced steadily towards our objectives until we reached a point within three- or four-hundred yards of Chocolate Hill. From this position our advance was continued by a series of "half-platoon" rushes. During the latter stages of this advance Major Fraser was killed. I then took over the command of 'A' and 'C' Companies.

Reaching the foot of Chocolate Hill, I found men of the 10th Division lying there three or four deep. Word was passed along for the Officer Commanding the Regiment that had just arrived. I therefore proceeded to where the message emanated and saw a Colonel of the Irish Fusiliers (he was wearing glasses and I omitted to ask his name) who had in his company a Major wearing the West African Medal Ribbon and whom the Colonel called Major Thompson or Johnston (or a similar sounding name). Being asked the nature of my orders by the Colonel, I told him that we were sent to support the 10th Division in the attack on the Hill. The Colonel then said his men were completely exhausted and could not proceed. On receiving this news, I replied that my men could not stay in their present position as they were exposed to heavy fire. At that same

79

time I notified him of my intention to "fix bayonets and take the Hill". I then gave the order for the Lincolns to fix bayonets and prepare to advance. After allowing sufficient time for my men to rest, I gave the order for the Lincolns to advance and then proceeded up the Hill.

Owing to the fact that the Naval Guns were still shelling the top of the Hill, I halted my Companies half way up and requested Lieutenant Gordon Hewart to signal the Naval Authorities our position. This he did and when the ships ceased firing we continued our advance. When we reached the top we discovered a trench occupied by the enemy. At this point we made contact with the other half of the Regiment – viz: 'B' and 'D' Companies – who in the meantime had advanced up the left side of the Hill. We then came in actual touch with the enemy and proceeded to do a certain amount of "mopping up" during which Lieutenant Webber was killed whilst jumping a trench. I then gave orders to my half battalion to make sangers with stones on the slopes of the Hill. While this was being done (it was now dark) a Major named Harrison of the Dublin Fusiliers came to me and asked if I was in command of the Lincolns, to which I replied, no, only half a battalion, he then said he was senior and would take command of the Hill.

Shortly after this Major Elkington came up the Hill and I reported to him what Major Harrison had told me, he then went and interviewed Major Harrison, during which there was an argument about seniority. On his return Major Elkington informed me that he was senior Officer and in command.

I may add that during the advance up the Hill with my half a battalion - the 10th Division did not take any part whatever – but remained at the bottom where I had found them after crossing the Salt Lake.

We maintained and consolidated our position during the night without any incident of moment. Towards dawn on the 8th, General Hill of the 10th Division came along and ordered me to retire; this I said was not possible without receiving definite orders from my Brigade. He thanked me and remarked that my men had done splendidly. Shortly after this our Adjutant Captain Hansen joined me, whereupon General Hill told him to withdraw, Captain Hansen replied that he could not do so – then in my presence the General gave him a written order to retire. It was now day-break and we commenced our retirement in extended order across the Salt Lake to Lala Baba. On my arrival here I was sent by General Maxwell to whom I explained fully, the situation.

## The Attack on Hill 'W': August 8th-9th

During the night 8th-9th we were ordered from Lala Baba to advance to a point on the left of Chocolate Hill. We arrived there just before day-break on the 9th and deployed to attack ('A' Company on the right) Hill "W".[17] We then continued our advance in extended order and soon came under heavy fire. We proceeded for about a thousand yards when Lieutenant Downs commanding my No. 1 Platoon reported he was in touch with the Staffords on his right. I went over to make quite certain and found the enemy marching in the same direction as ourselves. Although they were clothed in Khaki, I identified them owing to the fact that they were carrying coats rolled en-banderole. I then ordered Mr. Downs to wheel to his right and open fire, this he did and drove the enemy further to the right – No. 1 Platoon did a bayonet charge here, Mr. Downs being badly wounded and later died of wounds. After this skirmish we reformed and continued our advance on Hill "W". During this time we were under exceptionally heavy rifle and shell fire, consequently we were forced to continue our advance by forward rushes until we gained a point about three- or four-hundred yards from Hill "W". Here our casualties were very heavy. The enemy came down the slope of Hill "W" in extended order to attack us, I then ran along my front line in order to get my men ready to charge as soon as the enemy got near the high ground we were holding. I discovered that nearly all my men lying there were either killed or wounded. The enemy however did not continue their attack on us. Shortly after this Captain Lewis of 'C' Company asked if I had a spare field dressing for a man who was bleeding to death, whilst I was giving him this, Captain Lewis was shot in the side and killed. Immediately after this I was myself wounded. Sergeant Allport of my Company gave Captain Lewis a flake of Morphia before he died and then bandaged my wounds. As I could scarcely stand I came to the conclusion that I could not be any further service at the moment, so proceeded to make my way back to the rear assisted by my Company-Quartermaster-Sergeant and a private of the Border Regiment, both of whom were wounded like myself. The Border Regiment man was again hit on the way down and died at Romanoes Well near Chocolate Hill.

On my way from the front line I met the Officer Commanding the Border Regiment and also Major Marsh. After reporting the situation to them, I continued my journey to the Beach, arriving there in a state of exhaustion that I

---

[17] Hill "W" is another name for Ismail Oglu Tepe.

81

have no further recollection of anything until I found myself onboard a hospital ship, bound for Alexandria.

Before I left my advanced position the scrub had caught fire through the heavy shelling of the enemy.

P.S. This is the first time I have reported on the fighting at Gallipoli and hope any slight error in this record and the attached rough sketch, may be overlooked.

A.C. CROYDON, Lt.-Col.
8th Oct. 1930

# APPENDIX I

*ROLL OF HONOUR*

The following Roll of Honour commemorates the names of all those who gave their lives whilst serving with the 6th Battalion Lincolnshire Regiment during the Great War. Fatal casualties totalled 30 officers and 688 Other Ranks, equivalent to 17.5 per month of active service.

## OFFICERS

Box, Philip J.M., Lieut.
Browne, Percival L., Capt.
Cook, Robert L., 2/Lieut.
Cook, Thomas, 2/Lieut. (attd. from 12th Essex Regt.)
Downes, Gilbert C., Capt.
Fenwick, Anthony L., A/Capt.
Frere, Frederick J.H.T., Capt. M.C. (attd. from R.A.M.C.)
Fenwick, Anthony L., Capt.
Foster, John C., Capt. M.C.
Foster, Robert D., Lieut.
Fraser, D'Arcy M., A/Major (attd. from 75th Carnatic Infantry)
Frost, William E., Lieut. M.M.
Hewart, Gordon M., 2/Lieut.
Hornsby, Ridiard L., 2/Lieut.

Howis, Francis T., 2/Lieut. (attd. from 12th Essex Regt.)
Ingersoll, Hamilton, 2/Lieut.
Jones, Douglas L., A/Capt.
Lewis, John T., Capt.
Lockyear, Horace, 2/Lieut.
Margetts, Percy A., 2/Lieut.
Overton, Thomas D., Lieut.
Parkin, Thomas G., 2/Lieut.
Peake, Kenneth J.W., Lieut.
Read, Cyril De L., T/Lieut.
Stockdale, Norman H., 2/Lieut.
Thompson, Herbert B., T/Capt.
Webber, Lynden, T/Lieut.
Wilson, Alfred C., 2/Lieut.
Wickham, Lister D., T/Capt.
Wright, Vivian A.B., 2/Lt. (attd. from 12th Essex Regt.)

## OTHER RANKS

Ackrill, Frederick, Pte.
Adcock, Fred, Pte.
Addison, Robert, L/Sgt.
Allaway, Henry, Cpl.
Allett, Arthur, Pte.

Allis, John, Pte.
Allison, Ernest, Pte.
Altoft, Walter, Pte.
Ancliff, Frank E., Pte.
Anderson, Thomas, Pte.

Andrew, Thomas, Pte.
Andrews, Albert H., Pte.
Andrews, Arthur, Pte.
Andrews, Owen, Pte.
Armstrong, Ernest, Cpl.
Ashford, Charles, Pte.
Askew, Ernest, L/Sgt.
Aspland, Frank, Pte.
Atterby, George, Pte.
Ayling, Charles E., Pte.

Backhouse, Alfred W.H., Pte.
Bagley, Herbert, Pte,
Baildham, Ernest, Pte.
Bailey, William, Pte.
Baker, William, Pte.
Baldock, Frank, L/Cpl.
Baldock, George, Pte.
Ballance, Percy, Sgt.
Banyard, Ernest, L/Sgt.
Barber, Thomas, Pte.
Barker, George, Pte.
Barlow, Charles S., Pte.
Barlow, Francis E., Pte.
Barnes, Charles E., Pte.
Barnett, Walter S., Pte.
Barnfather, John, Pte.
Barrett, Samuel E., Pte.
Barrow, Leslie G., Pte.
Bastock, Frank, Pte.
Bateman, George, Pte.
Battram, Arthur E., Pte.
Bayles, Thomas H., Pte.
Bedell, Harry P., Pte.
Bedford, Charles, Pte.
Bedford, Harold, Sgt.
Bee, William J., Pte.

Beeson, Albert, Pte.
Bell, George, Pte.
Bellamy, Albert, Pte.
Bellamy, Fred, Pte.
Belt, Harold, Pte.
Belton, Herbert, Pte.
Bemrose, George, Pte.
Bennett, Frederick W., Pte.
Bennett, Paul, Pte.
Bennis, John T., Pte.
Benstead, Robert, L/Cpl.
Bentley, William, Pte.
Biggadike, Riley, Sgt.
Billson, George, Pte.
Birch, Robert C., Pte.
Birdsall, Percy, Pte.
Birkett, Harry J., Pte.
Blackburn, William H., Pte.
Blades, Alexander E., Pte.
Blakey, John W., Pte.
Bland, George, Pte.
Blaxhill, Joseph C., Pte.
Blyth, Percy G., L/Cpl.
Blythman, Arthur, Pte.
Boatwright, George, Pte.
Bodington, George E., Pte.
Bonner, Walter L., Pte.
Booth, Will, Pte.
Boston, John E., Pte.
Boswell, William, Pte.
Boultbee, William V., Cpl.
Boyfield, David, Pte.
Boyfield, Richard, Pte.
Brankling, Hector C., Pte.
Brannick, Albert H., Pte.
Brasier, George, L/Cpl.
Bratton, John T., Pte.

Brewitt, Arthur, C.S.M.
Briggs, Arthur, Pte.
Bristow, George, Pte.
Britton, Cyril F., Pte.
Brocklesby, Frederick, Pte.
Bromfield, John, Pte.
Brooks, George, Cpl.
Brothwell, Robert W., Pte.
Broughton, Harry, Pte.
Broughton, John W., Pte.
Brown, Arthur E., Sgt.
Brown, Frank, Pte.
Brown, Fred, Pte.
Brown, Leonard, Pte.
Broxholme, George F., Pte.
Bryan, George, Pte.
Buck, Frederick G., Pte.
Buckley, Jabez, Pte.
Burbidge, Joseph, Cpl.
Burgess, George H., Pte.
Burley, Joseph, Pte.
Burn, Jabez, Pte. M.M.
Burnett, Arthur, Pte.
Burnham, James, Pte.
Burrill David, Pte.
Burton, Archibald G., Pte.
Burton, Arthur, Pte.
Burton, George H., Pte.

Cadwallader, Herbert, Pte.
Cadwallader, William, Sgt.
Callaghan, Robert, Pte.
Calvert, Edgar W., Pte.
Carrott, Fred, Pte.
Carter, Arthur D., Pte.
Carter, George, Pte.
Carter, John E., Pte. M.M.

Caudwell, Charles, Pte.
Chambers, George, Pte.
Chapman, Edward, Pte.
Chappell, Robert, Pte.
Chase, William, Pte.
Chessum, Alfred J., Pte.
Christmas, Walter, Pte.
Church, Henry, Sgt.
Clapson, William H., Pte.
Clare, Frank, Pte.
Clark, Charles, Pte.
Clark, Clement, Cpl.
Clarke, Frank H., Pte.
Clarke, George, Pte.
Clarke, Reginald C., Pte.
Claxton, Frederick, Pte.
Clayton, Ernest A., Pte.
Cleary, Herbert P., Pte.
Clifton, Ewart P., Cpl.
Codling, Ernest, Pte.
Coe, Horace, Sgt.
Colclough, John, Pte.
Cole, Edward F., Pte.
Cole, William J., Pte.
Cole, William S., L/Sgt.
Colley, John H., Pte.
Collier, William, Pte.
Coman, Charles H., C.S.M.
Cook, George W., Pte.
Cook, Philip A., Pte.
Cooke, James, Pte.
Cooper, Robert J., Pte.
Cope, Frederick W., Pte.
Cordon, Thomas, Pte.
Costall, George, Pte.
Coult, Walter S., Pte.
Cox, George W., Pte.

Cozens, Arthur, Pte.
Cragg, Harry, Pte.
Creasey, Charles H., Pte.
Croft, Alfred H., Pte.
Croft, Thomas, Pte.
Crofts, Albert, Pte.
Cross, Charles L., Pte.
Crossland, Edward, L/Cpl.
Crouter, Frank, Pte.
Crowson, William A., Pte.
Cummins, William H., L/Cpl.
Cunnington, William C., Pte.
Curtis, Laurance T., Pte.
Cuthbert, James, Pte.
Cutler, James, Cpl.
Cutts, George W., Pte.

Dale, Ernest, Pte.
Dalton, William B., L/Cpl.
Dauber, William, Cpl.
Daubney, Edward R., Pte.
Daulton, William, Pte.
Dawson, Albert E., Cpl.
Dawson, Arthur M., Pte.
Day, Henry H., Pte.
Dean, Frederick, Pte.
Dennison, John, Pte.
Denniss, Arthur, Pte.
Dent, Charles, Pte.
Desborough, Willie W., Pte.
Devaney, Anthony, Sgt.
Devenish, Thomas H., Pte.
Dewe, Walter, Pte.
Ding, Walter, Sgt.
Dirkin, George, Pte.
Dodd, Harold, Pte.
Dodsworth, Frank, Pte.

Doyle, Joseph C., Pte.
Drayton, Percy W., Pte.
Drury, Thomas E., Pte.
Dunderdale, John T., Pte.
Dunderdale, Tom, L/Cpl.
Dyson, Arnold, Pte.

East, Alfred, Pte.
East, Ernest, Pte.
Eaton, Hermon, Pte.
Ebbage, David J., Cpl.
Edwards, John, Pte.
Edwards, Joseph W., Pte.
Ellis, Norman, L/Cpl.
English, Harry, Pte.
Espin, John W., Sgt.
Etty, Arthur, Pte.

Fawcett, Herbert, Pte.
Fawcett, John W., Pte.
Fawcett, William, Pte.
Fenwick, George H., Pte.
Fielding, Joseph, Pte.
Fields, Charles, Pte.
Fisher, John B., Pte.
Flavell, Joseph, Pte.
Fleming, William, Pte.
Flesher, William, Pte.
Fletcher, Walter, Pte.
Ford, Alfred, Pte.
Fountain, Thomas H., Pte.
Fowler, Ernest, L/Cpl.
Fowler, Thomas, Pte.
Fowler, Walter, Pte.
Fox, Frederick, Pte.
Fox, George, Pte.
Fox, James, L/Cpl.
Franklin, William H., Pte.

Franks, George P., Pte.
Fretter, Robert J., Pte.
Frost, Frederick J., Pte.
Futter, George, Pte.

Garner, Charles, Pte.
Garner, John R., Pte.
Garrett, Sidney, Pte.
Garrill, Fred, Pte.
Garwood, Eric J., L/Cpl.
Gascoyne, William, Pte.
Gee, George H., Pte.
George, James E., Pte.
Gibson, George W., Pte.
Gibson, James T., Pte.
Gillatt, Henry, L/Cpl.
Glover, Isaiah, Pte.
Goddard, George H., Pte.
Godley, Arthur, Pte.
Goldthorpe, Charles, Pte.
Good, James, C.S.M.
Goodwin, Charles S., Pte.
Gough, Thomas, Pte.
Graham, William H., Pte.
Green, Edward, Pte.
Green, Henry W., Pte.
Green, Percy A., Pte.
Green, Reginald W., Pte.
Greenfield, John W., Pte.
Gregory, Albert, Pte.
Gregory, Wilfred, Pte.
Grey, John, Pte.
Griffen, Moses, Pte.
Griffin, Ambrose, A/Cpl. D.C.M.
Grundy, Charles, Pte.

Hadfield, Thomas, Pte.
Hales, Walter, Pte.

Hall, Abraham, Pte.
Hall, Charles B., Pte.
Hall, Walter S., Pte.
Hallewell, Frederick, Pte.
Hamilton, Edward, Pte.
Harding, Esau, Pte.
Hargreaves, Henry J., Pte.
Harland, William, Pte.
Harper, Albert, Pte.
Harper, Allan, Pte.
Harris, Gilbert, Pte.
Harris, Harold P., Pte.
Harris, James E., Pte.
Harris, Walter G., Pte.
Harrison, John W., Pte.
Harrison, Tom, L/Cpl.
Hart, John, Pte.
Hart, Matthew H., Pte.
Hartshorn, Herbert, Pte.
Hayden, Victor W., Pte.
Hayes, Edward, Pte.
Haywood, Benjamin, Pte.
Hazeldon, Albert B., Pte.
Healey, Alfred, Pte.
Heath, Alfred, Pte.
Henshaw, William, Pte.
Herrett, Walter F., Pte.
Hewison, William, Pte.
Hewitt, Alfred, Pte.
Hewitt, Robert H., Pte.
Hiatt, Cyril E., Pte.
Hill, Charles, Pte.
Hill, George, Pte.
Hill, John W., Sgt.
Hill, Ralph G., Pte.
Hill, William, Pte.
Hill, William N., Pte.

Hitchcock, George A., Pte.
Hodge, John, Pte.
Hodgetts, Harold F., Pte.
Hodson, Fred, Pte.
Holey, Walter, Cpl.
Holland, Moses, Pte.
Hollingsworth, John W., Pte.
Holloway, Lester S., Pte.
Holmes, Arthur, Pte.
Holmes, Charles H., Pte.
Holmes, George, Sgt.
Holmes, Herbert, Pte.
Holmes, John W., Pte.
Hood, Harry R., Pte.
Hopson, George P., Pte.
Hornsby, Herbert, Pte.
Horswood, Edward, Pte.
Houltby, John R., Pte.
Hubbard, Thomas R., Pte.
Hudson, Benjamin, Pte.
Hudson, James G. M., Pte.
Hudson, Samuel, Pte.
Humphrey, Arthur T., Pte.
Hunt, George, Pte.
Hunt, James H., Sgt.
Hunt, William, Pte.
Hunter, George H., Pte.
Hutchins, Tom, Pte.
Hutchinson, Bertram, Pte.
Hyke, James E., L/Sgt.

Ingilby, Herbert C., L/Cpl.
Ismay, Joseph, Pte

Jackson, Albert, Pte.
Jackson, George, Pte.
Jackson, Tom, Pte.
Jackson, Walter H., Pte.

Jeanes, Frederick W., Pte.
Jenkins, Charles W., Pte.
Jessup, John R., Pte.
Johnson, Albert E., Pte.
Johnson, John R., Pte.
Johnson, Joseph E., Pte.
Jones, Harry, Pte.
Jones, Joseph, Pte.
Jones, William, Pte.
Juggins, Harry, Pte.
Kay, Abraham, Pte.
Kedge, Arthur C., Pte.
Keech, Arthur, Pte.
Kent, Edmund, Pte.
Kew, Charles W., Pte.
Key, George A., Pte.
Killick, Isaac, Pte.
King, Joseph, Pte.
Kinzer, Alfred, Cpl.
Kirkman, Ernest W., Pte.
Kirton, Arthur, Pte.
Kitchen, Alfred, Pte.
Knight, Luke, Pte.
Knipe, Charles, Pte.
Knipe, Francis H., Pte.
Knowles, George E., Pte.

Lambert, Ralph, Pte.
Lamming, William, Pte.
Lane, George A., Pte.
Lawrence, Frederick W., Pte.
Lawton, Frederick, Pte.
Leach, James W., Cpl. M.M.
Lear, Edward, L/Cpl.
Lee, Lewis, L/Cpl.
Lee, Harry, Pte.
Leek, William C., Pte.

Le Francios, Victor, Pte.
Leonardi, Ernest, Pte.
Levy, Atkin C., Pte.
Lewis, James E., Pte.
Loane, Henry W., Pte.
Locking, John G., Pte.
Long, Robert E., Pte.
Luddington, George F., Pte.
Lyman, John W., Pte.
Lyon, John W., L/Cpl.
Lyon, Thomas A., Pte.
Machray, Alexander A., Cpl.
Mackman, Richard, Sgt.
Maclaverty, Kenneth, Sgt.
Maclean, Peter, Pte.
Makins, Frederick E. B., Pte.
Marris, William, Cpl.
Marsden, Charles F., Pte.
Marsh, Frank, Pte.
Marshall, Albert, Pte.
Marshall, Frank, Pte.
Marshall, Frank Horace, Pte.
Martin, Arthur, Sgt.
Marwood, Charles H., Pte.
Mason, Alfred J., Pte.
McDonald Robert, Sgt.
McIntyre, Gordon, L/Cpl.
McMahon, Arthur, Pte.
McVarney, Edward, Pte.
Meadwell, Albert G., Pte.
Mears, Lawrence E., Pte.
Meatheringham, George A., Pte.
Mellership, Richard, L/Cpl.
Metcalfe, Leonard, Pte.
Mettam, George, Pte.
Middleton, James, Pte.
Miles, Herbert, Pte.

Mills, Charles H., Pte.
Milner, Frank, Pte.
Milson, Arthur, Pte.
Minton, William G., Pte.
Mitchell, Alfred J., Pte.
Montgomery, Sidney, Pte.
Moore, Benjamin, Pte.
Moore, George H.N., Pte.
Moore, James, Pte.
Moore, Thomas, Pte.
Morton, Aubrey, Pte.
Moseley, Herbert, Pte.
Moses, Richard, Pte.
Moss, Arthur, Pte.
Murphy, Albert E., Pte.

Needham, Charles, C.S.M.
Needham, Charles H., Pte.
Needham, George, Pte.
Neighbour, Henry W., Pte.
Nelson, George, Sgt.
Newborn, Charles S., Pte.
Newbould, Arthur, Pte.
Newbury, Charles T., Pte.
Nicholls, Charles, Pte.
Nicholson, George H., Pte.
Nicholson, John J., Cpl.
Norton, William, Pte.

Ogden, George, C.S.M.
Oliver, Herbert H., Pte.
Orme, John W., L/Cpl.
Overton, James W., Pte.
Oxby, Fred, Pte.
Parker, Donald, Pte.
Parker, Frank, Pte.
Parkes, William, Pte.
Parkin, George W., Pte.

Parkin, Tom, Pte.
Parrott, Thomas, Pte.
Parsons, Frederick, Pte.
Paterson, William, Pte.
Pearson, Joseph C., Cpl.
Pearson, John W., Pte.
Peck, Charles H., Pte.
Peck, John W., Pte.
Peesley, George, Pte.
Pegg, Joseph H., Pte.
Pell, Walter, Pte.
Pepper, John K., Pte.
Pestell, John, Pte.
Piggott, Anthony, Pte.
Pinney, Joseph, Pte.
Plowright, Ernest, Pte.
Pocklington, Arthur, Pte.
Pogmore, Harry, Pte.
Pollitt, John W., Pte.
Postle, John C., Pte.
Potter, Albert, Pte.
Powis, Harry, Cpl.
Poyser, John W., Pte.
Preece, Frederick C., Pte.
Preston, Fred, Pte.
Price, Henry, Pte.

Quipp, Joseph, Pte.

Raby, James, Sgt.
Radford, Sidney, Pte.
Ransome, Jess, Pte.
Rason, Charles, Pte.
Ratcliff, Leonard H., Pte.
Ratcliffe, Cyril, Pte.
Raybould, William, Pte.
Rayner, Harold, Pte.
Raynes, Luke, L/Cpl.

Revens, George S., Sgt.
Revill, William H., Pte.
Reynolds, Charles W., C.Q.M.S.
Rhodes, John, Pte.
Rice, Herbert C., Pte.
Riggall, Frank S., Pte.
Rimington, Thomas, Sgt.
Roberts, Henry H., Pte.
Roberts, Thomas A., Pte.
Robinson, Ernest, Cpl.
Robinson, Leonard, Pte.
Robinson, Stephen, L/Cpl.
Robinson, Walter, Pte.
Roe, Isaac H., Pte.
Roper, Charles E., Pte.
Roper, George, Cpl.
Rose, Henry W., Pte.
Rossington, George, Pte.
Rowbotham, Harold V., Pte.
Rowson, Charles, Pte.
Rudkin, John E., Pte.
Rushby, Charles H., Pte.
Russell, James, Pte.

Sargison, Charles, Pte. M.M.
Savage, Robert, L/Cpl.
Sawyer, Richard L., Pte.
Saxby, Percy, Pte.
Saxelby, Charles F., L/Cpl.
Scarborough, Charles, Pte.
Scorer, William, Pte.
Scott, George C., Pte.
Scott, George H., Pte.
Scott, Verdon, L/Cpl.
Scott, William H., Pte.
Searston, Arthur, Pte.
Sellars, Ernest W., Pte.

Sellars, William H. R., Pte.
Sewell, John E., Pte.
Sharman, Robert, Pte.
Sharp, Percy, Pte.
Shaw, John T., Pte.
Shaw, Clarence W., Pte.
Shearsmith, Harold, Cpl.
Shorrocks, Charles, Pte.
Short, Arthur, Pte.
Sismore, Fred, Pte.
Sismore, Harry, L/Cpl.
Skelton, Alfred, Pte.
Skupham, Walter, Pte.
Slater, Tom A., L/Cpl.
Sleaford, Harry, Pte.
Smallman, Joseph, Pte.
Smith, Ben, Pte.
Smith, Charles, Pte.
Smith, Frederick, Pte.
Smith, George W., Pte.
Smith, Harry (b. Clarborough), Pte.
Smith, Harry (b. Burgh), L/Cpl.
Smith, Harry (b. Leicester), Pte.
Smith, John W., Pte.
Smith, Philip St.G. D., Pte.
Smith, Thomas (b. Lincoln), Pte.
Smith, Thomas (b. Spalding), Pte.
Smith, Walter, Cpl.
Snee, John, Pte.
Snow, George, Pte.
Soole, Stanley W., Pte.
South, Joseph, Pte.
Sparks, Walter P., Pte.
Speechley, Ernest, Pte.
Speechley, Harry, Pte.
Speight, Walter, Pte.
Spencer, George H., Pte.

Spink, William J., Sgt.
Spray, George, Pte.
Stacey, Thomas W., L/Sgt.
Stainton, Robert S., Pte.
Staley, Samuel, Pte.
Staley, Walter, Pte.
Staniland, Joseph, Pte.
Stapleton, Maurice, Pte.
Steel, Bernard S., Pte.
Stennett, Edward, Pte.
Stennett, Percy E., Pte.
Stephenson, Albert, Pte.
Stokes, Cecil, Pte.
Stott, Horace F., Pte.
Stout, James, Pte. D.C.M.
Straw, Henry, Pte.
Stubley, John E., Pte.
Styles, George, Pte.
Summerfield, John W., Pte.
Swift, Herbert, Pte.
Swinger, Walter, Pte.
Sykes, John, Pte.
Sylvester, Joseph, Pte.

Tarpey, Thomas H., Sgt.
Tasker, Ernest, Pte.
Taylor, Benjamin, L/Cpl.
Taylor, Fred, L/Cpl.
Taylor, Henry, Pte.
Taylor, Joseph, Pte.
Taylor, John. S/Sgt. (attd. from R.A.O.C.)
Taylor, Thomas H., Pte.
Teece, Leonard, Pte.
Temple, Arthur, Pte.
Temple, Harry, Pte.
Tester, William, Sgt.

Thompson, Charles, Pte.
Thompson, John, Pte.
Thompson, John W., Pte.
Thompson, Joseph, Pte.
Thompson, William H., Pte.
Thornton, Charles, Pte.
Tighe, John, Sgt.
Tingle, William, Pte.
Todman, William, L/Cpl. M.M.
Tomlinson, Alfred, Cpl.
Toplis, Bertie, Pte.
Toyn, Charles, Pte.
Toyne, Fred, Pte.
Treadwell, Arthur, L/Cpl.
Trafford, Thomas C., Cpl.
Troughton, Frederick, Pte.
Tucker, Frank O., Pte.
Turnell, Herbert, Pte.
Turner, Henry, Pte.
Turner, Sydney M., Pte.
Tutin, Harry, Sgt.
Twinn, John E., Cpl.
Tyers, Walter, Pte.

Upton, William, Pte.

Varey, Frederick H., Sgt.
Venables, John, Pte.
Vessey, Ernest L., Pte.

Waddington, William, Pte.
Waite, George H., Pte.
Waite, Thomas, Pte.
Wakefield, Charles C., L/Cpl.
Walker, George, Pte.
Walker, Walter, Pte.
Walker, William J., Pte.
Wallis, Charles, Pte.

Walpole, George F., Pte.
Walton, Robert W., L/Sgt.
Wand, Robert, L/Cpl.
Ward, George, Pte.
Ward, Leslie J., Pte.
Ward, Lawrence A., Sgt.
Wareham, William, Pte.
Wass, Francis E.H., Pte.
Waterfield, Harold, Pte.
Watson, Archer, Pte.
Wattam, Herbert H., L/Cpl.
Waumsley, Charles E., Pte.
Webb, Ernest, Pte.
Webb, William J.W., Pte.
Webster, Bertram O., Pte.
Welberry, Walter, Pte.
Welch, Robert, Pte.
Welham, Henry B., Pte.
Wescott, Elton H., Cpl.
Wesseldine, William R., Pte.
West, Fred, Pte.
West, George, Pte.
Westoby, Harry B., L/Cpl.
Wetton, Edward, Pte.
Wheatley, Ernest, Pte.
Whelpton, Wilfred H., Pte.
Whelton, Charles, Cpl.
White, Frank, L/Cpl.
Whitelock, James J., L/Cpl.
Whiting, William H., Cpl.
Whitley, John W., Pte.
Whyley, George, Pte.
Whymant, Amos F., Pte.
Wilde, Charles W., Pte.
Wilkinson, George, (b. Ulceby) Pte.
Wilkinson, George (b. Bentley) Pte.
Wilkinson, John, Pte.

Wilkinson, John W., Pte.
Willerton, John D., Pte.
Williams, John T., Pte.
Willoughby, Ernest, Pte.
Wilson, Alfred, Sgt.
Wilson, Frank, Pte.
Wilson, Frederick, Pte.
Wilson, Frederick W., Pte.
Wilson, George W., Pte.
Wilson, James A., Pte.
Wilson, Stanley, Pte.
Wood, George, Pte.
Wood, Joseph, Pte.
Wood, William, Pte.

Wooddin, Benjamin, Sgt.
Woodhead, Luther, Pte.
Woods, Charles W., L/Cpl.
Woodward, Alfred, Pte.
Wool, Benjamin J., Pte.
Wray, George H., Pte.
Wright, Arthur, Pte.
Wright, George H., Cpl.
Wright, Osborn, Pte.
Wright, Walter, Pte.

Yates, Walter H., L/Sgt.
York, William, Pte.

# APPENDIX II

## HONOURS AND AWARDS

### VICTORIA CROSS

<u>41788 Cpl. (L/Sgt.) Arthur Evans (alias Walter Simpson)</u>

*For most conspicuous bravery and initiative when with a daylight patrol sent out to reconnoitre and to gain touch with a neighbouring division. When on the west bank of a river an enemy machine-gun post was sighted on the east bank. The river being too deep to ford, Sgt. Simpson volunteered to swim across, and having done so crept up alone in rear of the machine-gun post. He shot the sentry and also a second enemy who ran out; he then turned out and caused four more enemy to surrender.*

*A crossing over the river was subsequently found, and the officer and one man of his patrol joined him, and reconnaissance was continued along the river bank. After proceeding some distance, machine-gun and rifle fire was opened on the patrol and the officer was wounded. In spite of the fact that no cover was available, Sgt. Simpson succeeded in covering the withdrawal of the wounded officer under most dangerous and difficult conditions and under heavy fire.*

*The success of the patrol, which cleared up a machine-gun post on the flank of the attacking troops of a neighbouring division and obtained an identification, was greatly due to the very gallant conduct of Sgt. Simpson.*

<u>Capt. Percy Howard Hansen, Adjutant</u>

*For most conspicuous bravery on 9th August, 1915, at Yilghin Burnu, Gallipoli Peninsula. After the second capture of the "Green Knoll" his Battalion was forced to retire, leaving some wounded behind, owing to the intense heat from the scrub which had been set on fire.*

*When the retirement was effected Captain Hansen, with three or four volunteers, on his own initiative, dashed forward several times some 300 to 400 yards over open ground into the scrub under a terrific fire, and succeeded in rescuing from inevitable death by burning no less than six wounded men.*

## DISTINGUISHED SERVICE ORDER

<u>Lt.-Col. Gerald Trevor Bruce (attached)</u>
London Gazette 03/06/1918:  No citation.

<u>T/Capt. Francis Ponsonby Duck</u>
London Gazette 02/02/1916:
*For his excellent leadership of 'D' Company in the attack upon Hill 53[18] on the night of the 8th August 1915.  After his Company Commander was wounded he pushed on in the face of considerable losses and immediately attacked and captured the 'Circular Work' on the summit of the hill - being the first of the British troops to enter the work.  He acted entirely on his own initiative and the successful capture of the hill was largely due to him.  During the action of the 9th August he behaved admirably when his energy and bravery were beyond all praise.*

<u>Maj. George Henry Gater, D.S.O. (attached)</u>
London Gazette 17/09/1917:
*For conspicuous gallantry and devotion to duty.  He led his battalion with brilliant skill and resolution during an attack, minimising their casualties during three days' intense shelling by his able dispositions and good eye for ground. He directed the consolidation, and remained in command for three days, although severely wounded in the face early in the action.*

<u>Capt. (T/Maj.) Percy Howard Hansen, V.C., M.C.</u>
London Gazette 16/09/1918:
*For conspicuous gallantry and devotion to duty.  He volunteered to carry out a reconnaissance, and brought back valuable information obtained under heavy artillery and machine gun fire, which had been unprocurable from other sources.  Throughout he did fine work.*

<u>T/Capt. Thomas Douglas Sutherland, M.C.,</u>
London Gazette 26/09/1917 (details published 09/01/1918):
*For conspicuous gallantry and devotion to duty.  He led his company with great gallantry in the attack, but on reaching his objective found his flank exposed*

---

[18] Hill 53 is another name for Chocolate Hill.

*owing to the troops on his right having been unable to advance. He immediately went back, rallied a company which had lost heavily in officers and senior N.C.O's, and led them forward to their objective. He then organized a defensive flank and made the position secure. He showed the greatest courage and leadership, and it was entirely owing to his initiative and determination that the advance of his battalion was successfully carried out.*

T/Maj. Thomas Douglas Sutherland, D.S.O. M.C. (Second Award Bar)
London Gazette 02/04/1919 (details published 10/12/1919):
*For conspicuous gallantry and initiative during operations on the 6th and 7th November 1918, on the east bank of Grande Honnelle River. His battalion was held up in an attack by mist and heavy machine-gun fire, and suffered severe casualties, but by his personal courage, fine example and skilful dispositions, he was able to inspire all ranks with his own splendid fighting spirit, and to hold on at a most critical period for a day, taking the leading companies forward the following day and capturing the position.*

## MILITARY CROSS

2/Lt. Arthur Claude Backham
London Gazette 10/12/1919:
*He did very gallant and useful work with his platoon, acting as a fighting patrol when the battalion successfully captured Hem-Lenglet on the 10th October, 1918. He worked forward under heavy machine-gun and rifle fire and established a post, where he held on till dusk. Later, he entered the village and assisted at the capture. On his way his platoon encountered a machine-gun post of the enemy. The post was rushed, the garrison killed and the machine gun captured. It was mainly due to the initiative of this officer, who appreciated the enemy's weak point and succeeded in establishing a strong forward flank position, that the operation was successful.*

Rev. Richard Langley Barnes (attd. from R.A.C.D.)
London Gazette 16/07/1918 Birthday Honours List.
*For Services in the Field.*

T/Capt. Wilfred Douglas Mayhew Bone
London Gazette 26/07/1918:
*For conspicuous gallantry and devotion to duty when in command of a raiding party. He first dealt with a trench mortar, which was actively retaliating, and when the team refused to surrender he demolished the whole shaft with a mobile charge. Then, guiding his men, he demolished four dugouts and a machine gun, and was largely instrumental in the capture of fourteen prisoners and one machine gun. He set a magnificent example to the men all through the enterprise.*

T/Capt. Arthur Cecil Burrows
London Gazette 14/11/1916:
*For conspicuous gallantry in action. He led his company with great gallantry and determination, his prompt support of the brigade being of great value. He set a splendid example to his men.*

T/Lt. Robert Hugh Clay
London Gazette 04/06/1917:
*For distinguished services in the Field.*

T/Capt. Leslie Charles Crick
London Gazette 10/12/1919:
*He did exceptionally fine work on the night of 6th/7th October, 1918, when his company made a successful attack on the village of Aubencheul-au-Bac. By personal reconnaissance, he succeeded in obtaining sufficient information to get his company through the enemy wire and to occupy the village and establish posts on the Canal de la Sensée during the night.*

T/Capt. Albert Charles Croydon, D.C.M.
London Gazette 02/02/1916:
*For exceptional conduct on the night of the 8th August 1915 during the attack on Hill 53, and for his exceptional leadership and initiative during the action of August 9th , until being wounded.*

2/Lt. George Frederick Devaliant, 3rd Bn. (attd. 6th)
London Gazette 10/12/1919:

*He was in command of the company which successfully attacked the village of Hem-Lenglet on the 10th October, 1918, taking one officer and eleven other ranks prisoner, capturing four machine-guns and inflicting about fifty casualties on the enemy. Throughout the operation he made his dispositions and commanded his company with great skill and gallantry, leading them in the actual attack.*

T/Capt. John Cecil Foster
London Gazette 17/09/1917:
*For conspicuous gallantry and devotion to duty. At great personal risk he made several crossings across an open space under heavy shell fire in order to keep up the telephonic communication with his battalion headquarters. His fearlessness and energy in dealing with the situation when it was becoming obscure through lack of information were most valuable.*

Capt. Percy Howard Hansen, V.C. D.S.O.
London Gazette 29/10/1915:
*For conspicuous gallantry at Suvla Bay on 9th September, 1915. He made a reconnaissance of the coast, stripping himself and carrying only a revolver and a blanket for disguise. He swam and scrambled over rocks, which severely cut and bruised him, and obtained some valuable information and located a gun which was causing much damage. The undertaking was hazardous. On one occasion he met a patrol of 12 Turks who did not see him, and later a single Turk whom he killed. He returned to our lines in a state of great exhaustion.*

Quartermaster & Hon. Capt. Phillip Henry Jones
New Years Honours List. London Gazette 01/01/1918:
*For valuable service rendered in connection with the War.*

2/Lt. Walter Sydney Peel
London Gazette: 07/03/1918:
*For conspicuous gallantry and devotion to duty in an attack. He took command of a party whose officer had been wounded and led them forward to the capture of an important strong point. Later, when he was the only officer left, he took charge of the company and organised the consolidation. Throughout the whole operation he displayed great coolness and leadership.*

*Fig. 16: Captain Hansen wins the Military Cross.*

### T/Lt. Eric Springfield Playle
London Gazette 17/09/17:

*For conspicuous gallantry and devotion to duty during a hostile counter-attack. He displayed boundless energy in collecting and organising Lewis guns and teams, moving from post to post under heavy enemy rifle fire, and personally supervising every detail of the defence. He set a very fine example of fearlessness, and did work of the utmost value for a continuous period of several days.*

### T/Capt. Carl Joseph Shephard
London Gazette 26/07/1918:

*For conspicuous gallantry and devotion to duty when in command of the first wave of a raiding party. He reached the exact objective allotted to him, and by pressing close to the barrage, enabled the waves to enter the trenches before the enemy could direct their machine-gun fire. The first to enter the trenches, he kept his men under control, covered the withdrawal, and was the last of his party to leave. His leadership and courage greatly inspired all ranks.*

### 2/Lt. Thomas Douglas Sutherland
London Gazette 14/11/1916:

*For conspicuous gallantry in action. He led several bombing attacks with great courage and determination. Later, he assumed command of his company, and set a splendid example of his men throughout.*

### Lt. William Edward Tolley
London Gazette 10/12/1919:

*He did excellent work whilst in command of his company in the fighting on the 7th November, 1918. His company was engaged in the attack on the railway east of the Grande Honnelle River. In face of strong opposition, he advanced his company down to the west bank and established it there. He held on to his position during the whole day, showing great gallantry and ability to command.*

## DISTINGUISHED CONDUCT MEDAL

#### 9/13781 Sgt. H. Boardman
London Gazette 25/11/1916:
*For conspicuous gallantry in action. He held a bombing post alone, throwing bombs at the enemy, and was largely instrumental in checking their advance.*

#### 11604 L/Cpl. Arthur Henry Breese
London Gazette 16/11/1915:
*For conspicuous bravery and devotion to duty on the 9th August 1915, at Suvla Bay (Dardanelles), when he volunteered to go out with an officer of his regiment under very heavy fire, to assist in rescuing six wounded men from the burning scrub. It was an attempt involving the greatest risk, and the wounded were saved from almost certain death. L/Cpl. Breeze displayed a courage and devotion beyond all praise.*

#### 3/5381 Cpl. (A/Sgt.) Joseph Burton
London Gazette 03/03/1917:
*For conspicuous gallantry in action. He displayed great courage and initiative when in charge of a post, and was instrumental in capturing six prisoners. He has previously done fine work.*

#### 16491 Sgt. Charles J. Dexter (Barrowden)
London Gazette 03/09/1918:
*For conspicuous gallantry and devotion to duty when in a raid he led his men with great spirit and determination to the second objective. He was here wounded, but continued to fight until he collapsed. His courage and disregard of danger were an inspiring example to his men.*

#### 41788 Sgt. Arthur Evans V.C. (Bolton)
London Gazette 02/12/1919:
*For great courage and initiative near Cambrai. He was in charge of a Platoon acting as a fighting patrol on the night of the 6th/7th October 1918, with instructions to clear the country north of the Château of Aubencheul-au-Bac to the Canal de la Sensée. A strong enemy post was encountered. He promptly rushed the post, killing ten, wounding several and taking one prisoner. The*

*prisoner secured most valuable information. He has shown excellent leadership and the utmost disregard of all danger.*

## 7603 A/Cpl. Ambrose Griffin
London Gazette 15/03/1916:
*For conspicuous gallantry at Suvla, Gallipoli Peninsula, on 3rd December 1915 when he went out, unarmed and unaided, some sixty yards in front of our trenches, and brought in one after the other, the bodies of an Officer and a Sergeant. He had twice previously been driven back by the enemy's sniping fire.*

## 10274 Pte. G.A. Hall (Bungay, Norfolk)
London Gazette 22/10/1917:
*For conspicuous gallantry and devotion to duty. During an attack he rushed on in front of his Platoon and bombed the enemy's trench and dug-outs, until he was himself wounded in the head. This prompt and gallant action demoralised and scattered the enemy, and materially assisted in securing the objective.*

## S/9106 L/Cpl. (A/Sgt.) Thomas Ernest Harrison
London Gazette 03/03/1917:
*For conspicuous gallantry in action. He led a party into the open under heavy fire, and succeeded in capturing five prisoners. He set a splendid example throughout.*

## 8115 Pte. Charles Frederick Jones
London Gazette 21/06/1916:
*For conspicuous gallantry and consistent good work.*

## 5935 A/C.S.M. Harry Alfred Jackson
London Gazette 21/06/1916:
*For consistent good work and devotion to duty.*

## 7312 Sgt. George Patience M.M. (Burn)
London Gazette 03/09/1918:
*For conspicuous gallantry and devotion to duty when in a daylight raid he reorganised the men in the captured line and refused to go back despite having been twice wounded and being in great pain. He greatly assisted in the success of the operations, and by his personal example inspired his comrades.*

### 8485 Sgt. Arthur Sleight M.M. (Scunthorpe)
London Gazette 03/09/1919:
*Both as an organiser and as a fighting N.C.O. throughout a long period of continuous service in the field he has proved his excellence, and is a most valuable and reliable N.C.O. As company Lewis gun Sergeant he has trained his Lewis gunners to a high state of efficiency. His constant cheerfulness and readiness to volunteer for any dangerous work have been a great example and incentive to the men of his company, to which he is a great asset.*

### 10642 Pte. James Stout (Sutterton)
London Gazette 11/03/1916:
*For conspicuous gallantry at Suvla Bay on 21$^{st}$ and 22$^{nd}$ August 1915. Lance-Corporal Taylor and Private Stout went out in front of the line during the day to take water to wounded men. Between them they brought back no less than five wounded men in broad daylight and under heavy fire.*

### 10642 Pte. James Stout D.C.M. (Second Award Bar)
London Gazette 25/08/1917:
*Conspicuous gallantry and devotion to duty as stretcher-bearer. When nearly all the garrison of a strong point were killed and wounded he organised and carried out the evacuation of the wounded, making several journeys himself under heavy shell fire. Finally, he returned when all the wounded had been brought in and made a further thorough search of the shelled area. His splendid example of devotion and fearlessness greatly inspired all the other stretcher-bearers, who were ready to follow him anywhere.*

### 9409 C.S.M. (A/R.S.M.) Thomas Arthur Stuart (Aston-under-Lyne)
London Gazette 17/04/1918:
*For conspicuous gallantry and devotion to duty. He has rendered valuable service during a long period, making his influence felt throughout the battalion. His courage and coolness in action have been most marked.*

### 8624 Cpl. (A/Sgt.) William Algernon Tapsell (Abbey Wood)
London Gazette 17/09/1917:
*For conspicuous gallantry and devotion to duty in assisting to dig out nineteen men who had been buried in a dug-out by a gas shell. Finding it impossible, owing to the darkness, to work in a gas helmet, at imminent risk of his life he*

removed his own, and by his efforts successfully extricated some of the men. The dug-out was full of lethal gas fumes, and six of the men affected subsequently died. He set a splendid example of fearless devotion and self-sacrifice.

### 8624 Cpl. (A/Sgt.) William Algernon Tapsell D.C.M. (Second Award Bar)
London Gazette 17/09/1917:
*For conspicuous gallantry and devotion to duty when in command of Battalion Scouts. Having been ordered to reconnoitre in front of our advancing patrols, his party came under heavy and unexpected rifle and machine gun fire. In spite of this, however, after warning the patrols behind him, he continued to push forward until, owing to several casualties, further advance was impossible, whereupon he withdrew very skilfully with all his wounded back to our lines. Throughout the action he displayed splendid coolness and presence of mind and an utter disregard of personal safety.*

### 9858 L/Cpl. (A/Sgt. Shoemaker) Charles Ducey Taylor
London Gazette 11/03/1916:
*For conspicuous gallantry at Suvla Bay on 21st and 22nd August 1915. Lance-Corporal Taylor and Private Stout went out in front of the line during the day to take water to wounded men. Between them they brought back no less than five wounded men in broad daylight and under heavy fire.*

### 9978 C.S.M.  Frederick Wrightson
London Gazette 25/08/1917:
*For conspicuous gallantry and devotion to duty in leading his Company during an advance, although knocked over and partly buried by a shell. His fine example was most inspiring to his men, over whom he has always had remarkable control and power of leadership.*

### MERITORIOUS SERVICE MEDAL

| | |
|---|---|
| Holberry, Joseph, R.Q.M.S. | Rofe, Albert V., Sgt. |
| Hubbard, Thomas, Sgt. D.C.M. | Rogers, Herbert, A/Cpl. M.M. |
| Pickwell, Edward, Cpl. | Stock, George, R.S.M. |
| Reynolds, William, Pte. M.M. | |

MILITARY MEDAL & BAR
Handsley, Will, Sgt.
Holt, James W., L/Cpl.

MILITARY MEDAL

Adcock, Charles, Pte.
Allington, Leonard A., Pte.
Andrews, William A., Pte.
Barchard, Arthur, Pte.
Bavin, George, Pte.
Bothamley, John J., Pte.
Beck, William, Pte.
Burn, Jabez, Pte.
Carter, John E., Pte.
Carver, Frank, Pte.
Clay, Albert V., Sgt.
Chester, David, Pte.
Coulson, George H., Pte.
Dawson, Harold, Pte.
Delury, William S., Pte.
Dickens, George R., Pte.
Field, Joseph E., Pte.
Gibbons, Albert E., Pte.
Goodman, Thomas H.F., Pte.
Goulsbra, William T., Cpl.
Griffin, William, Pte.
Hartshorne, Joseph, Pte.
Hartung, Charles S., Sgt.
Hempsall, Robert, Pte.
Horton, Albert E., Cpl.
Houghton, William H., Cpl.
Jaques, George T., Pte.
Kibble, Thomas H., Pte.
King, Walter, Pte.
Leach, James W., Cpl.
Lyon, James, Pte.
Maltby, Percy, Pte.

Marchant, George, Sgt.
Maxey, Harry, Cpl.
McIver, Sidney E., Pte.
McNally, Herbert C., Pte.
Melton, Sydney A., Cpl.
Mosses, William J., Cpl.
Newman, Edward A., Pte.
North, Thomas, Sgt.
Parks, Herbert, Pte.
Patience, George, Pte.
Pease, Frederick, Cpl.
Phillipo, Sydney F., L/Cpl.
Reynolds, William, Pte.
Robinson, Benjamin, Pte.
Rogers, Herbert, Sgt.
Sargison, Charles, Pte.
Shields, Tom, Pte.
Simkin, Frederick C., Pte.
Sleight, Arthur, Sgt.
Smith, Arthur, Pte.
Sparrow, George, Pte.
Stalley, Charles C., Pte.
Staples, James, Sgt.
Tapsell, William A., Cpl.
Todman, William, L/Cpl.
Topham, John R., Pte.
Trafford, George W., Pte.
Underwood, Thomas E., Pte.
Walker, William, Cpl.
Watson, Edward, Sgt.
White, James, Pte.
Wilkinson, Joseph, Pte.

Wilson, John H., Sgt.

Woods, John, Sgt.

Wright, Horace W., Pte.

## MENTIONED IN DESPATCHES

Barnard, Reginald J., Cpl.

Breese, Arthur H., Pte. D.C.M.

Cannel, Frank S., T/Capt.

Croydon, Albert C., T/Capt.

Duck, Francis P., Capt.

Fenwick, Anthony L., 2/Lt.

Foster, John C., T/Capt.

Gater, George H., Lt.-Col. D.S.O.
(attached)

Hansen, Percy H., B/Maj. V.C.,
D.S.O., M.C.,

Phelps, Malet P., Lt.-Col.

Sutherland, Thomas D., T/Maj.

## CROIX DE GUERRE (FRENCH)

Hansen, Percy H., Capt.

North, Thomas, Sgt. M.M.

# APPENDIX III

*11TH (NORTHERN) DIVISION*

The 11th (Northern) Division came into existence on 21st August 1914, under Army Order No. 324, which authorised the formation of the first six new Divisions of Kitchener's Army. The Division was composed of early wartime volunteers and assembled at Belton Park near Grantham in September 1914. By late spring 1915, the recruits were judged to be ready for active service, and the Division was consequently ordered to reinforce the beleaguered garrison on Gallipoli. It sailed for the Mediterranean in June and July 1915 and formed part of the Suvla Bay landing force at Gallipoli on August 7th 1915. It continued to serve at Gallipoli until the evacuation of Suvla in December. After a period of time in Egypt, the Division was transferred to the Western Front and served there from the Battle of the Somme in 1916 until Armistice. On 28th June 1919, the Division was officially disbanded, having sustained more than 32,100 casualties during the war.

## ORDER OF BATTLE

<u>32nd BRIGADE</u>
9th Bn. West Yorkshire Regiment
6th Bn. East Yorkshire Regiment *(left 18/01/1915 to become Divisional Pioneers)*
2nd Bn. Yorkshire Regiment *(joined 14/05/1918)*
6th Bn. Yorkshire Regiment *(left 18/05/1918)*
6th Bn. York and Lancaster Regiment
8th Bn. Duke of Wellington's Regiment *(joined 18/01/1915; disbanded 13/02/1918)*
32nd Brigade Machine Gun Company *(formed March 1916, moved into 11th M.G. Bn. 28/02/1918)*
32nd Trench Mortar Battery *(joined 17/07/1916)*

## 33rd BRIGADE
6th Bn. Lincolnshire Regiment
6th Bn. Border Regiment *(disbanded 09/02/1918)*
7th Bn. South Staffordshire Regiment
9th Bn. Sherwood Foresters Regiment
33rd Brigade Machine Gun Company *(formed March 1916, moved into 11th M.G. Bn. 28/02/1918)*
33rd Trench Mortar Battery *(joined July 1917)*

## 34th BRIGADE
8th Bn. Northumberland Fusiliers
9th Bn. Lancashire Fusiliers *(disbanded 21/02/1918)*
8th Bn. Duke of Wellington's Regiment *(transferred to 32nd Bde. 18/01/1915)*
5th Bn. Dorset Regiment *(joined 18/01/1918)*
11th Bn. Manchester Regiment
34th Brigade Machine Gun Company *(formed March 1916, moved into 11th M.G. Bn. 28/02/1918)*
34th Trench Mortar Battery *(joined July 1917)*

## DIVISIONAL TROOPS
6th Bn. East Yorkshires Regiment (Pioneers) *(joined 18/01/1915)*
250th Machine Gun Company *(joined 16/11/1917, joined Divisional M.G. Battalion 28/02/1918)*
No. 11 Machine Gun Battalion *(created 28/02/1918)*
No. 11 Motor Machine Gun Battery *(joined early 1915, left when Division moved to Gallipoli)*
11th Divisional Motor Ambulance Workshop *(absorbed by Divisional Train when Division moved to Gallipoli)*

## DIVISIONAL MOUNTED TROOPS
A Squadron, Royal Glasgow Yeomanry *(joined 02/06/1915, left 30/06/1915)*
B Squadron, 1st Hertfordshire Yeomanry *(joined 04/04/1916, left July 1916)*
11th Divisional Cyclist Company *(formed January 1915, left 12/07/1916)*

## DIVISIONAL ARTILLERY
LVIII Brigade, R.F.A.
LIX Brigade, R.F.A.
LX Brigade, R.F.A. *(disbanded 5-13/02/1918)*
LXI (H) Brigade, R.F.A. *(left Division on embarkation for Gallipoli)*
CXXXII Brigade, R.F.A. *(joined 26/04/1916 in Egypt as a Howitzer Brigade, broken up 25/01/1917)*

11th (Hull) Heavy Battery, R.G.A. *(a Battery of 4 4.7-inch guns which left the Division before embarkation for Gallipoli and joined XXXVIII Heavy Artillery Brigade)*
11th Divisional Ammunition Column
V.11 Heavy Trench Mortar Battery R.F.A. *(joined 09/08/1916, left 12/02/1918)*
X.11, Y.11 and Z.11 Medium Mortar Batteries R.F.A. *(joined 09/08/1916; on 03/02/1918 was Z broken up and batteries reorganised to have 6 x 6-inch weapons each)*

ENGINEER UNITS
67th Field Company, R.E.
68th Field Company, R.E.
86th Field Company, R.E.
11th Divisional Signal Company, R.E.

FIELD AMBULANCES
33rd Field Ambulance, R.A.M.C.
34th Field Ambulance, R.A.M.C.
35th Field Ambulance, R.A.M.C.

ANCILLARY UNITS
11th Divisional Train A.S.C. (112th, 113th, 114th and 115th Coys). *(This train did not sail for Gallipoli. It joined the 26th Division on 01/04/ 1916, and was replaced by the Companies of the 53rd Divisional Train.)*
213th Divisional Employment Company *(joined by 30/06/1917)*
22nd Mobile Veterinary Section
21st Sanitary Section *(left 09/12/1916, for IV Corps Sanitary Area, Fifth Army)*

DIVISIONAL COMMAND
| | |
|---|---|
| Major-General F. Hammersley | 22/08/1914 |
| Major-General E. Fanshawe | 23/08/1915 |
| Lieutenant-General Sir C. Woollcombe | 04/07/1916 |
| Brigadier-General J. Erskine | 01/12/1916 (Acting) |
| Major-General A. Ritchie | 05/12/1916 (wounded) |
| Major-General H. Davies | 09/05/1917 (wounded 13/09/1918) |
| Brigadier-General O. Winter | 13/09/1918 (Acting) |
| Major-General H. Davies | 13/10/1918 |

# BIBLIOGRAPHY

Middlebrook, M., *Your Country Needs You: Expansion of the British Army Infantry Divisions: 1914-1918,* Pen & Sword, 2000.

Nalson, David, *The Poachers: The History of the Royal Lincolnshire Regiment 1685-1969*, The Trustees of the Royal Lincolnshire Regiment Museum, 2003.

*Operation Report of 6th Lincolns for the 9th August 1915,* WO 95/4299 pt. 47 & 48, Crown copyright material held by The National Archives.

Simpson, Maj. Gen. C.R., *The History of the Lincolnshire Regiment 1914-1918*, The Medici Society, 1931.

*Soldiers Died in the Great War 1914-1919: Part 15: The Lincolnshire Regiment*, J.B. Hayward & Son, 1989.

*Suvla Bay: Report on the landing, by Capt. A.C. Croydon, 6th Battalion. Lincolnshire Regiment,* CAB 45/228, Crown copyright material held by The National Archives.

*War Diary of the 6th Battalion Lincolnshire Regiment*, WO 95/1817, Crown copyright material held by The National Archives.

# INDEX

**Frederick Gordon Spring** C.B., C.M.G., D.S.O., was commissioned into the Lincolnshire Regiment in May 1898 and served with the Regiment during the Boer War. He retired from the army as a Major in 1907, only to be recalled for service at the outbreak of the First World War. During this time he served as an Embarkation Officer for a brief period but he was soon posted to the Staff of the 33rd Brigade as Brigade Signalling Officer. It was in this capacity that he served alongside the 6th Lincolns before being wounded at Gallipoli. In June 1916 he was promoted to Acting Lt.-Colonel, and took command of the 11th Battalion, Essex Regiment. In September 1918 he returned to the 33rd Brigade as its Brigadier-General. After the war he remained with the Lincolnshire Regiment and went on to command the 1st Battalion between 1923 and 1927.